"Pastor Mark Jones has written an admirable treatise on the heart of biblical ethics: the virtues of faith, hope, and love. His book is based firmly on Scripture, and he has arranged it as a catechism: questions, answers, and commentary. He also digs deep into classic theological expositions, especially among the Puritans. This arrangement, clearly and vividly written, enables readers not only to understand these teachings, but to internalize them, and thus to grow in grace. This book will be a great help to individual and family devotions and to adult Bible study groups. I hope that many will have the opportunity to read it to the glory of God in Christ."

John Frame, professor of systematic theology and philosophy emeritus, Reformed Theological Seminary, Orlando

"Much writing on Christian spirituality is hollow, bereft of theological heft and awash in baptized therapeuticism. By contrast, *Faith. Hope. Love.* is weightily Puritanesque in the best sense—offering clear, Christ-centered, scriptural ballast for the Christian life. Rooted richly in the Reformed tradition, Jones walks us through the theological virtues and the shape they give to our life in Christ. More importantly, in each chapter he points us to the Christ in whom we place our faith—the one we imitate in love and for whom we wait in hope. I highly commend this work."

Derek Rishmawy, columnist, *Christianity Today*; cohost, *Mere Fidelity* podcast

"The old paths are the way into the future. Mark Jones knows this is true for the life and witness of the church of Jesus Christ. He takes us back to the medieval theological virtues, organizes them in a reformational catechism, and uses post-Reformation, orthodox theological distinctions, all to instruct our minds, enflame our hearts, and move us to service. This is as clear as it gets when it comes to the doctrine of justification by faith alone and all that it means for living out a life of faith, hope, and love."

Daniel R. Hyde, pastor, Oceanside United Reformed Church, Carlsbad/Oceanside, California; adjunct instructor of ministerial studies, Mid-America Reformed Seminary; author, *Welcome to a Reformed Church*

"The questions we ask can be just as important as the answers. Well-meaning Christians often harmfully express the three theological virtues of faith, hope, and love in sentimental tropes devoid of substance. I will be recommending Mark's excellent book for many to use devotionally. Its catechismal format has provided a superb corrective, moving us to delight in Christ-centered faith, hope, and love, and what they require of us in response."

Aimee Byrd, author, *Housewife Theologian*; *Theological Fitness*; and *No Little Women*

"In this useful work, Jones clearly and practically guides the reader into the virtues of the body of Christ. The book is laid out in catechetical format, which Jones employs with great dexterity. The questions are those that the *fides quaerens intellectum* ('faith seeking understanding') of any believer naturally poses to itself, and the definitions that follow by way of response are elegant and comprehensive. The expositions of the answers are doctrinally profound but expressed very simply and memorably. Steeped in the wisdom of the doctors and the great Puritan guides of the heart, *Faith. Hope. Love.* is a much-needed map of the path of the Christian's walk with God."

Peter Escalante, fellow of rhetoric, New St. Andrew's College

"Mark Jones puts to rest the lie that scholasticism is arid and boring. In a rich display of biblical text, respect for the past, and pastoral sensitivity, *Faith. Hope. Love.* gives to the church a summary of biblical virtue to help us live our theology in honor of a Savior who loves us so faithfully. This is a worthy addition to Jones's other works that have made the best of the Great Tradition accessible and enjoyable for a wide Christian audience."

Ian Hugh Clary, assistant professor of historical theology, Colorado Christian University; coeditor, *Pentecostal Outpourings: Revival and the Reformed Tradition*; senior fellow, Andrew Fuller Center for Baptist Studies

Faith. Hope. Love.

Faith. Hope. Love.

The Christ-Centered Way
to Grow in Grace

MARK JONES

WHEATON, ILLINOIS

Cover design: Jorge Canedo Estrada

First printing 2017

Printed in the United States of America

Scripture quotations are from the ESV® Bible (The Holy Bible, English Standard Version®), copyright © 2001 by Crossway, a publishing ministry of Good News Publishers. Used by permission. All rights reserved.

All emphases in Scripture quotations have been added by the author.

Trade paperback ISBN: 978-1-4335-5566-4
ePub ISBN: 978-1-4335-5569-5
PDF ISBN: 978-1-4335-5567-1
Mobipocket ISBN: 978-1-4335-5568-8

Library of Congress Cataloging-in-Publication Data

Names: Jones, Mark, 1980– author.
Title: Faith, hope, love : the Christ-centered way to grow in grace / Mark Jones.
Description: Wheaton : Crossway, 2017.
Identifiers: LCCN 2017001883 (print) | LCCN 2017036673 (ebook) | ISBN 9781433555671 (pdf) | ISBN 9781433555688 (mobi) | ISBN 9781433555695 (epub) | ISBN 9781433555664 (tp)
Subjects: LCSH: Theological virtues—Miscellanea. | Theology, Doctrinal—Popular works.
Classification: LCC BV4635 (ebook) | LCC BV4635 .J66 2017 (print) | DDC 234/.2—dc23
LC record available at https://lccn.loc.gov/2017001883

Crossway is a publishing ministry of Good News Publishers.

VP		27	26	25	24	23	22	21	20	19	18	17
16	15	14	13	12	11	10	9	8	7	6	5	4	3	2	1

For fathers who have taught me
about faith, hope, and love:

Joel R. Beeke
Richard B. Gaffin Jr.
J. I. Packer

Contents

PART 3 LOVE

Questions 31–57

Preface

Yet [the demons] neither hope nor love. Instead, believing as we do that what we hope for and love is coming to pass, they tremble. Therefore, the apostle Paul approves and commends the faith that works by love and that cannot exist without hope. Thus it is that love is not without hope, hope is not without love, and neither hope nor love are without faith.

Augustine, *Enchiridion*

And he called the name of the first daughter Jemimah, and the name of the second Keziah, and the name of the third Keren-happuch. And in all the land there were no women so beautiful as Job's daughters. And their father gave them an inheritance among their brothers.

Job 42:14–15

So now faith, hope, and love abide, these three; but the greatest of these is love.

1 Corinthians 13:13

Faith, hope, and love have been referred to as the three divine sisters. I like to think of them as three beautiful sisters (like Job's daughters), joined hand in hand, dancing around in a circle together. Eventually, the one sister, love, separates from faith and hope and forever dances alone, while faith and hope vanish from

13

the scene. That picture may appear odd until we realize that faith and hope were there to help love on her way until she was mature enough to be alone. For she exists as the greatest of the sisters and deserves the preeminence, just as Christ remains the greatest of the sons of men and deserves the same.

Faith, hope, and love are also referred to as the *theological virtues*. The whole Christian life, in terms of our living in response to God and his new work in us, springs from faith, hope, and love. Everything we do as Christians relates to these three virtues.

This triad appears frequently in the New Testament, perhaps even more so than we might realize. Besides the well-known passage in 1 Corinthians 13:13, Paul refers to this triad twice in his first letter to the Thessalonians:

> . . . remembering before our God and Father your work of faith and labor of love and steadfastness of hope in our Lord Jesus Christ. (1 Thess. 1:3)

> But since we belong to the day, let us be sober, having put on the breastplate of faith and love, and for a helmet the hope of salvation. (1 Thess. 5:8)

Elsewhere, Paul writes to the Galatians, "For through the Spirit, by faith, we ourselves eagerly wait for the hope of righteousness. For in Christ Jesus neither circumcision nor uncircumcision counts for anything, but only faith working through love" (Gal. 5:5–6; see also Rom. 5:1–5; Eph. 4:2–5; Col. 1:4–5). Besides Paul, the author of Hebrews and the apostle Peter also highlight the triad of faith, hope, and love (Heb. 6:10–12; 1 Pet. 1:3–8).

Surprisingly, there are fewer books devoted to this subject than we might expect, especially given the importance of these virtues in the Christian life. Augustine (354–430) wrote the *Enchiridion: On Faith, Hope, and Love* in response to a request by a man named

Laurentius. It is a sort of manual on Christian living that follows a catechetical structure. Subsequent theologians developed their own approach to the three virtues, all of them making many valuable and lasting contributions.

Peter Lombard (ca. 1096–1160) in book 3 of *The Sentences* (*On the Incarnation of the Word*) also offers some valuable insight on this topic. Thomas Aquinas (1225–1274), one of the truly great theologians of the church, includes a significant section on faith, hope, and love in his *Summa Theologiae*. Godefridus Udemans (ca. 1581–1649), an influential Dutch Nadere Reformatie ("further Reformation") divine, penned *The Practice of Faith, Hope, and Love* (1612), which considers the Apostles' Creed (faith), the Lord's Prayer (hope), and the Ten Commandments (love) as ways to understand the theological virtues. Finally, John Angell James (1785–1859) contributed a somewhat unknown but very plain and pastoral book, *The Christian Graces: Faith, Hope and Love*.

There are others but, as far as I am aware, nothing recent from a Reformed perspective on the three theological virtues. Of course, there are no shortage of works on faith, but few treat hope and love alongside faith. This, I think, is a pity, since each virtue informs the other. We can learn much about faith from hope and love, just as we can learn much about love from faith and hope.

In this book I have attempted to do something a little different from what one finds in most books geared toward Christian laypeople. I have included at the beginning of each chapter a question and answer, with a twofold purpose:

1. To write a catechism on "faith, hope, and love"
2. To help answer specific questions in relation to the theological virtues

Catechetical instruction was a major part of instruction in the early church and Reformation eras. It had its place in the medieval church too, though it was generally restricted to the training of the clergy. The proliferation of catechisms in the Reformation and post-Reformation eras was a sign of health in the church. The "prince of the Puritans," John Owen, hoped that more catechisms and confessions would be written over the course of church history. In the eighteenth century, many English Baptist pastors would write their own catechisms upon entering the ministry, but today the practice of writing catechisms is almost unheard of—and possibly assumed to be a little dangerous for those who find Westminster hard to improve on.

The writing of a catechism on faith, hope, and love is important, I believe, because it allows us in our present context to ask the right questions in order to achieve the right answers. As any counselor knows, the questions are as important as the answers. There are, naturally, other questions and answers that could have been asked and answered in relation to this topic. This book by no means seeks to be exhaustive. But I have tried to give readers a glimpse into these virtues as a sort of starting point for further inquiry.

In my section on love, for example, I have tried to state positively what love requires. Many in the past have looked at love from the perspective of the Ten Commandments, which is ideal and proper in my view. In one respect, I have followed this order, but I have also tried to state the issue positively (i.e., what is required) rather than negatively (i.e., what is forbidden). Many people misunderstand the proper use of the law and so do not see the benefits of the law of God. We think of the "don'ts" instead of the "dos." I am hoping that my approach to the law, which is our expression of love toward God and our neighbor, will give us a renewed appreciation for God's commandments.

I am also persuaded that Christians, especially in the Western world, do not focus on our biblical hope as much as we should, in part because we live fairly comfortable lives. Hope is present in our thinking, but it does not occupy our hearts, souls, and minds as much as it should. Christian hope rises in glory where hardship exists on earth. At the very least, then, we should be aware of the doctrine of hope and should seek to cultivate a more hopeful expectation of that which God promises us in his Word.

As for faith, much has been written and continues to be. I freely acknowledge my intellectual debt to such Puritan luminaries as John Owen and Thomas Goodwin on this topic. They have taught me more than anyone else that our faith as a grace does more than act as an instrument for receiving salvation. There exists a past, present, and future component to our faith in this life. Much of what I seek to ask and answer was utterly lost on me early in my Christian life. But reading the Puritans and the Reformers helped me to understand the glory of faith in ways I had never dreamed possible. The questions and answers in part 1, on faith, are designed to help us better appreciate this remarkable gift that God gives us.

These theological virtues are graces given to us from a gracious God. With faith, hope, and love, we may say to the God and Father of our Lord Jesus Christ in response to his promises, "A threefold cord is not quickly broken" (Eccles. 4:12).

Part 1

FAITH

Question 1

What is the worst sin?

The worst (and first) sin is unbelief.

In the beginning God made the world good—indeed, very good once woman had been made to complement man (Gen. 1:31). But Adam and Eve sinned in their unbelief, and God could no longer say that everything was very good. Unbelief, not pride, was the first sin. Adam and Eve were tempted to doubt God's words to them, including his warning of consequences (Gen. 3:1, 4). Then they were induced to pride, wishing to become like God (Gen. 3:5).

Since then, unbelief has ruined countless souls. In Noah's day, the world turned a deaf ear to the "herald of righteousness" (2 Pet. 2:5). Because of their obstinacy, they drowned. Since the prevailing sin of God's people in the exodus was unbelief (Ps. 95:7–8; Hebrews 3), they died in the wilderness (Num. 26:65). Those miraculously redeemed out of Egypt could not enter the Promised Land because of unbelief (Heb. 3:19). In the New Testament, we even read of Christ marveling at two things in particular:

1. The faith of the Roman centurion (Matt. 8:10)
2. The unbelief of his own people in Nazareth (Mark 6:6)

Imagine causing the Son of God, "in whom are hidden all the treasures of wisdom and knowledge" (Col. 2:3), to marvel!

In the world today, the sin of unbelief continues to abound beyond measure. People do not believe what God has to say through his Son—the living, trustworthy voice of God. Little do they know and understand that the world's problems can be solved relatively easily. They can exchange their unbelief for faith in God and Christ. In one respect, it is so easy for us because it was so hard for someone else. In another respect, it is so difficult because the most important and valuable thing in the world (i.e., that we believe) is a free gift (Matt. 11:25–27; 16:17; John 1:12–13; 6:44; 1 Cor. 12:3; Gal. 1:16; Eph. 1:11; 2:8; Phil. 1:29). How do we convince people that the most valuable thing in the world is free?

The faith that God requires sorts everything out. Our problems, fears, sins, and anxieties are solved by faith. This explains why God is so concerned about whether we have faith. Faith is a powerful little thing (Matt. 17:20). As weak as it can be, this gift from God conquers all because of the Conqueror to which it unites us (Matt. 14:31).

Mixed with our faith, however, remains a great deal of unbelief waging war against our souls. We believe, but we hate our unbelief. We Christians know how much our unbelief hinders us, and we feel its crippling effects daily. How often do we wish that God would simply give us more faith and not more money or success or friends? But do we really want more faith? Are we prepared for how this affects our lives in a world plagued with sin, misery, and unbelief? Perhaps we understand all too well what greater faith will do to us and thus are content to live with as little faith as possible. Having great faith is dangerous. Ask Abraham. Ask Christ.

Unbelief remains at the heart of our sin and our love for sin. So while we struggle to believe, we also enjoy our unbelief to some extent. This is the problem: God has to repeatedly convince his people that faith is always the better way, even if it is the most painful way. Unbelief is easy and thus also enticing. But unbelief, of all sins, has to be mortified by the Spirit (Rom. 8:13). The Christian sensitive to his sin acknowledges that a mass of infidelity still remains in our renewed nature. As the Puritan John Ball confesses in his excellent work on faith,

> O Lord, I am grossly ignorant of your ways, doubtful of your truth, distrustful of your power and goodness, disobedient to your commandments. You have given rare and excellent promises in your holy Word, but I inquire not after them, rejoice not in them, cleave not unto them in truth and steadfastness, settle not my heart upon them, make them not my own, keep them not safe.[1]

Unbelief is no small sin but rather the greatest of all sins. It gives birth to all our other sins. Or to put the matter more vividly, unbelief essentially tells God to shut up, because we do not want to hear what he says. Just as faith brings us to God (Heb. 11:6), so unbelief causes us to run from God.

He is "grieved" by unbelief. In fact, nowhere is this more plainly demonstrated than in Christ's words to his disciples. On the road to Emmaus, what is it that grieves Christ? Unbelief: "And he said to them, 'O foolish ones, and slow of heart to believe all that the prophets have spoken!'" (Luke 24:25). After that, Jesus appears to the eleven and again questions their unbelief: "And he said to them, 'Why are you troubled, and why do doubts arise in your hearts?'" (Luke 24:38). He practically chastises Thomas for believing only because he has seen the risen Christ (John 20:29).

Christ himself is the remedy against the guilt and power of sin. Thus, in our unbelief, we sin against the remedy. Nothing, then, is more serious than unbelief, whether for Christians or non-Christians. Nothing will debilitate us more than unbelief.

Why do people pray so little? Because they do not really believe the promises God makes to them regarding prayer. How many prayers have been strangled to death by unbelief?

Why do people depart from God? Because of their unbelief (Rom. 11:20; Heb. 3:12).

Why do people lie? Because they do not really believe that God is present, listening and caring about their falsehood.

Why do people worry? Because in unbelief they want to be in control rather than to trust in God's providential care of their lives whereby he works all things together for good to those who love him (Rom. 8:28).

Why are people so self-sufficient? Because in their unbelief they think that they do not really need God. Very often, the worst poison made from our sinful hearts is that of self-sufficiency, for it keeps us from God.

As Spurgeon once said, "Faith is like Samson's hair but on the Christian; cut it off, and you may put out his eyes—and he can do nothing."[2] Before we can begin to appreciate the value of faith, we must understand the heinousness of unbelief. Then and only then can we desire the remedy. And let us be clear about one thing: this is not a matter that should unsettle only unbelievers. As believers, we should be deeply concerned about our unbelief and the duty placed on us to rest more and more on the one who is Faithful and True (Rev. 19:11).

Question 2

What is saving faith?

Saving faith is the Spirit-enabled embrace of and resting on our faithful God in Christ for the redemption offered by him through the promise of the gospel.

A question so vitally important seems almost impossible to answer in one respect. When we try to define *faith*, we are left feeling as though more needs to be said. Indeed, given the supernatural character of faith (Eph. 2:8) and its importance in the Christian life (Heb. 11:6), we can be grateful for this seemingly incomplete definition. Can we, who live by this principle (Rom. 1:17), ever fully understand in this life what it means to have faith? If we could, we would have not faith but sight. Living by faith means moving into a realm whereby we are uncertain of ourselves but more certain of God and his faithfulness. Faith relinquishes self-dependence for dependence on one whom we can never fully grasp or understand. Who would ever dare to do this?

Those in the Bible who exhibit faith are secure and confident in God. As the psalmist says, "I believe that I shall look upon the goodness of the LORD in the land of the living!" (Ps. 27:13). Believers must be firm in their faith:

If you are not firm in faith,
>   you will not be firm at all. (Isa. 7:9)

Long before the author of Hebrews described faith as "the assurance of things hoped for, the conviction of things not seen" (Heb. 11:1), the Old Testament writers conveyed this same understanding of faith. As Job says,

For I know that my Redeemer lives,
>   and at the last he will stand upon the earth.
And after my skin has been thus destroyed,
>   yet in my flesh I shall see God,
whom I shall see for myself,
>   and my eyes shall behold, and not another.
My heart faints within me! (Job 19:25–27)

And,

I smiled on them when they had no confidence,
>   and the light of my face they did not cast down.
>   (Job 29:24)

How else can Job say these words if he does not have "assurance of things hoped for" and "conviction of things not seen"? But what he hopes for and what he is convicted of are realities that require something supernatural working in Job. His faith is something special: it is a gift from above, which causes him to hope in the one who will come from above.

The person who lives with assurance and possesses godly conviction because of his faith in God is contrasted with the proud person who is self-assured and trusts in himself: "Behold, his soul is puffed up; it is not upright within him, but the righteous shall live by his faith" (Hab. 2:4). Self-sufficiency and faith are enemies of each other.

Faith, then, is not simply (or merely) assent to the truth God has revealed (cf. James 2:19). Rather, it denotes the radical principle by which man thinks and acts in relation to God and man. God looks for this kind of faith: a firm and unwavering confidence based on an ingrained attitude of trust in him (cf. Num. 14:11, "How long will this people despise me? And how long will they not believe in me, in spite of all the signs that I have done among them?"). Faith and trust go hand in hand (Ps. 78:22).

The New Testament presents a multifaceted concept of faith. Personal faith may be placed in doctrines, in words spoken, or in persons. With the arrival of Christ on the scene of redemptive history, faith leading to salvation becomes a dominant focus on the pages of the New Testament.

Believing assent emerges as a clearly prominent theme in the New Testament witness. For example, when Jesus heals the ill son of an official, he says, "Go; your son will live"; in response, "the man believed the word that Jesus spoke to him and went on his way" (John 4:50). The official went beyond assenting to Christ's promissory exhortation by immediately trusting (taking) him at his word, even before he could get home to lay eyes on his miraculously healed son.

In the case of the Roman centurion, we have an example of such remarkable faith in Christ's ability and power to heal that even Jesus marveled when the centurion affirmed that just a word would heal his paralyzed servant who was not with him (Matt. 8:5–13). Like Abraham, the centurion had faith in what God was able to do.

Sometimes the New Testament highlights an explicitly soteriological element in connection with faith. For example, Paul informs the Thessalonians that they were beloved by the Lord because the Father chose them to salvation "through sanctification by the Spirit and belief in the truth" (2 Thess. 2:13). This same faith trusts in the "powerful working of God" (Col. 2:12).

While we are to believe the truth, the predominant New Testament focus is believing on a person—namely, Christ Jesus—and his work. Thomas Watson exclaims, "The promise is but the cabinet, Christ is the jewel in it which faith embraces."[1]

Jesus is the one "whom God put forward as a propitiation by his blood, to be received by faith" (Rom. 3:25). We are to place our faith in Christ, who satisfies the wrath of God hanging over our heads. This point is exemplified in John 3:18: "Whoever believes in him is not condemned, but whoever does not believe is condemned already, because he has not believed in the name of the only Son of God." Christ himself is the ground of our faith: "For in Christ Jesus you are all sons of God, through faith" (Gal. 3:26). Elsewhere Paul speaks to the Ephesians of their "faith in the Lord Jesus" (Eph. 1:15; cf. Col. 1:4; 1 Tim. 1:14; 2 Tim. 1:13).

When we believe on Christ, we also trust in God as the object of our faith. As Christ says in the Upper Room Discourse, "Let not your hearts be troubled. Believe in God; believe also in me" (John 14:1). Elsewhere Christ declares, "Truly, truly, I say to you, whoever hears my word and believes him who sent me has eternal life. He does not come into judgment, but has passed from death to life" (John 5:24). Since God works through Christ by his Spirit, believing in Jesus takes us to God, and trusting in him means believing in the one he sent to save us from our peril and damnation. Christ's authority and power are gifts given to him from above, which means we trust in what God is able to do through his Son. Denying Christ means rejecting the Father and vice versa (John 10:22–30).

Regrettably, many today think of faith merely as that which procures from God and Christ what they want, namely, salvation. While that is true—gloriously true—we must remember that faith is not just the way a Christian begins his life but also the way he lives his life. The regulative principle of the Christian life is faith in

God and Christ, for "the righteous shall live by faith" (Rom. 1:17). (Let the reader note that throughout this book, by saying God and Christ, I am making use of the common manner of speaking in the New Testament where God often refers to the Father and is distinguished from the God-man; see 1 Cor. 8:6; 15:15, 27; 2 Cor. 13:14.)

Because of what Christ has done, nothing less than utter commitment to him will suffice for a Christian. There are no 50 percent (or even 99 percent) Christians. We are wholly (100 percent) committed to Christ. Please do not get me wrong. I am not saying that our faith or our obedience flowing from it is 100 percent pure and without any unbelief. I am saying that even the weakest, sin-tainted faith receives and rests totally on Christ alone. We either believe with and from our whole heart, or we do not believe at all. And yet we can all say that though we believe, we also pray that God would help our unbelief (Mark 9:24).

Hebrews 11:1–12:2 is to the New Testament what Genesis 22 is to the Old. At the beginning, we are given the definition of faith as "the assurance of things hoped for, the conviction of things not seen" (Heb. 11:1). Knowledge is essential to faith, for we must believe that God exists (v. 6). Faith looks to God's promises (v. 6, "he rewards those who seek him"). Faith also leads to obedience (v. 8). It is, as I have said above, the radical principle of our obedience. But it does not consist in obedience. Rather, the heart looks to the invisible God (v. 27), knowing that he is faithful (v. 11). Faith goes against the wisdom of the world because God's ways are always better than what the world can offer (vv. 24–26). Faith has value because we trust not in ourselves but in God. Those with faith, whether strong or weak, were still saved by the Passover Lamb because the object remained the same for both the "strong" believer and the "weak" believer (v. 28).

The virtue of faith in the New Testament, then, consists in clinging to and resting on the faithful God. He shows his faithfulness through his Son, whom we must look to because he is the "founder and perfecter of our faith" (Heb. 12:2). By the Spirit, we lean on God and Christ because of what they alone are able to offer us. Thus we can have both assurance and conviction, because faith brings us to God.

Question 3

Where does faith come from?

Faith, while a human act, comes from God
as a supernatural and empowered gift.

Free grace and faith have a special relationship to one another. God grants faith as a gift (Eph. 2:8), yet he does not believe for us.[1] Each believer must do just that—believe. In this way, God's sovereignty and man's responsibility are involved in the accomplishment of faith. Theologians have developed a number of important distinctions in the matter of faith and salvation in order to safeguard both the gracious way of salvation and the integrity of human action in the process of salvation (see Gal. 2:20).

One such way of understanding faith as the gift of God resulting in the belief of a person is the act-habit (or act-power) distinction. God grants us the supernatural gift of faith (the habit/power) so that we can believe the supernatural truths of the gospel (the act). A natural faith, of ourselves, would allow us to rise no higher than natural theology, which cannot save. God grants the power, but we perform the act. As John Flavel observes, "Though faith (which we call the condition on our part) be the gift of God, and the power of believing be derived from God; yet the act of believing is properly our act."[2]

In other words, merely possessing the habit of faith will not lead to our justification; we must also carry out the act of faith. To be sure, anyone possessing the habit will perform the act. Likewise, while the habit enables us to believe, we must really believe. It truly is our act, our faith. This idea helps us to affirm with Paul the necessity of the "obedience of faith" (Rom. 16:26).

God freely gives the "habit" of faith to us by the Holy Spirit working it in us. As Peter Bulkeley argues, "The habit is freely given us, and wrought in us by the Lord himself, to enable us to act by it, and to live the life of faith; and then we having received the gift, the habit, then (I say) the Lord requires of us that we should put forth acts of faith."[3]

We are passive when God grants us the habit of faith. But once we receive it, we who are enabled to believe become "active" in our expression of faith. We are no longer dead wood but living trees. This distinction has an important relationship to our union with Christ.

The act of the will completes the union between Christ and the believer, which makes the believer ultimately one with him. However, as the bride, we are simply confirming a union that has taken place. So, contrary to the common view of marriage, which requires the consent of both partners since a man (usually) cannot marry a woman against her will, the spiritual union on Christ's part to his bride does not require assent from the sinner "because," says Thomas Goodwin, "it is a secret work done by his Spirit, who does first apprehend us before we apprehend him."[4] That is, Christ establishes a union in time with the elect sinner by "apprehending" him or her and then giving the Spirit to him or her. But this union is only complete (i.e., an "ultimate union") when the sinner exercises faith in Christ. Goodwin adds,

It is true indeed the union on Christ's part is in order of nature first made by the Spirit; therefore Phil. 3:12, he is said first to "comprehend us before we can comprehend him"; yet that which makes the union on our part is faith, whereby we embrace and cleave to him. . . . It is faith alone that does it. Love indeed makes us cleave to him also, but yet faith first.[5]

The act and habit of faith precede the act and habit of love. Our faith is that act whereby we knowingly cleave to our Savior. Faith alone, not love or good works, does this. We can speak of Christ "taking," "apprehending," and "comprehending" the sinner. According to Goodwin, Christ "takes hold of us before we believe" and "works a thousand and a thousand operations in our souls to which our faith concurs nothing. . . . Christ dwells in us and works in us, when we act not and know not our union, nor that it is he that works."[6] Before new believers are aware, our Lord unites them to himself (i.e., "takes hold of" them) and works in them.

As Herman Witsius says,

By a true and real union, (but which is only passive on their part,) [the elect] are united to Christ when his Spirit first takes possession of them, and infuses into them a principle of new life: the beginning of which life can be from nothing else but from union with the Spirit of Christ. . . . Further, since faith is an act flowing from the principle of spiritual life, it is plain, that in a sound sense, it may be said, an elect person is truly and really united to Christ before actual faith.[7]

The elect are united to Christ when his Spirit takes possession of them and gives them new life (i.e., regeneration). Union with Christ precedes actual faith, but "mutual union" is active and operative. The "mutual union" is thus emphasized not only by the act of faith in the sinner but also by the fact that the benefits of Christ for his people (e.g., justification, adoption, and sanctification) flow out of this union.

Pastorally speaking, we can note many advantages to the act-power distinction in relation to union with Christ. First, the faith that justifies is really ours and truly acts as the instrument of justification, whereby we receive the forgiveness of sins and righteousness of Christ by imputation. We must be careful to state that it is not our faith that justifies but God through our faith, without which we cannot be justified.

Second, the faith that justifies is enabled by the power (*habitus*) that God freely (graciously) grants to us, apart from works. Without this gift, our "acts" of faith would be carnal and lifeless. Our belief in God and Christ would possess no true spirituality. Hence, we avoid the antinomian error whereby Christ believes for us, mere passive "blocks" for whom he believes. We also avoid a legalistic error by contending that we possess no natural capacity for faith. Justification is an irrevocable act of God, because he formed the habit of faith himself. God imputes to us Christ's righteousness because our act of faith is the instrument for receiving full justification (Westminster Confession of Faith [WCF] 11.2). Justification depends entirely on God while at the same time demanding our faith to obtain it.

Third, in relation to union with Christ, we hold that he first graciously embraces us and then enables us to embrace him in the act of believing. Only when this is done are we justified through our "ultimate union" with Christ. But we only unite ourselves to him because he first united himself to us. We love him because he first loved us.

Fourth, we must remember that our acts of faith toward Christ never end. They are lifelong. Faith is not a one-time event but an ongoing and "busy little thing."[8] Reflecting on Ephesians 3:17 ("so that Christ may dwell in your hearts through faith"), Goodwin observes that our acts of faith relate to Christ dwelling in our hearts:

For Christ to dwell in us by faith is that there may be a continual eyeing of Christ, and acting on Christ by us, as an object who has virtue to convey into us and to come in upon our hearts, and work upon our souls; . . . for Christ to dwell in our hearts by faith is by operation and working, whereof faith is the instrument.[9]

Indeed, while some may be uncomfortable with saying that we "receive Jesus into our hearts," the concept is biblical (see John 1:12) and is something we do all our lives in our daily acts of faith. According to Goodwin, through faith, "Christ is said to dwell in the soul, by letting him into the soul and into the heart, and affecting the heart with him."[10] Dispositions of love will arise in our hearts when we put forth acts of faith in our Lord.

Question 4

What does it mean that
faith is supernatural?

That faith is supernatural means that it cannot
be experienced according to the natural order of
things, specifically the natural ability of man.

If the formal object of faith is the God who is faithful (Heb. 11:11), theologians have called the material object of faith the Word of God, apart from which there can be no active faith. John Calvin claims that there is a "permanent relationship between faith and the Word."[1] Francis Turretin also writes some memorable words regarding the relationship between faith and the Word of God:

> The first question may seem hardly necessary among Christians who should consider as an incontrovertible truth the fact that the Scriptures are inspired of God (*theopneuston*) as the primary foundation of faith. Yet even among Christians of this age, there are too many atheists and libertines who endeavor in every way to weaken this most sacred truth. Therefore it is of the greatest importance to our salvation that our faith should

be in good time fortified against the diabolical cavils of these impious persons.[2]

Not much has changed since the seventeenth century. Some believe the Scriptures to be the primary foundation of faith, and others weaken (or aim to destroy) this sacred truth.

The supernatural revelation that comes from the mouth of God provides the external means for believers who possess the Holy Spirit to be "illuminated." We are not illuminated apart from objective truth, but objective truth has no value to us unless it is accompanied by supernatural illumination. Faith arises from the authority and truth of God in the Scriptures. The apostle Paul makes this point himself: "But this I confess to you, that according to the Way, which they call a sect, I worship the God of our fathers, believing everything laid down by the Law and written in the Prophets" (Acts 24:14).

We believe the Scriptures are the Word of God because of the internal testimony of the Holy Spirit, who illumines our hearts to such truth. We can be infallibly assured of their divine origin because of the divine operation of the Spirit. Faith must be based on true knowledge, but faith must be Spirit wrought so that it recognizes and loves God's truth.

While we can never comprehend God, we can still possess true knowledge of him. J. I. Packer notes, "As far as our thoughts about him correspond to what he says about himself, they are true thoughts about him, and constitute real knowledge about him. . . . [A]nd this knowledge he himself gives us by his own verbal self-testimony."[3] We attain such knowledge of God through the Scriptures by the supernatural illumination of the Holy Spirit. Before the formation of the canon (our "rule" of faith—the Scriptures, including the Old and New Testaments), God communicated to his prophets by way of direct revelation. Such communication, such as God commanding Abraham to sacrifice his son, possessed divine power and efficacy that infallibly assured the recipient that God was speaking.[4] Nevertheless, God required Abraham to exercise his "faith, conscience, obedience, and reason" in order to know that God had indeed spoken to him.[5]

One needs supernatural faith to believe supernatural revelation. A natural faith cannot ascend so high as to infallibly believe God's testimony concerning himself and particularly the person and work of Jesus Christ. Thus, Owen argues, "If we believe it not with faith divine and supernatural, we believe it not at all."[6] Nothing is more difficult for us to believe than that a Jewish man died for our sins on a cross and that he is none other than the divine Son of God. Jonah in a big fish is easier to believe than the truths of the gospel.

An internal, efficacious work of the Holy Spirit must illuminate the minds of believers so that they not only recognize the divine authority of Scripture but also embrace the truths it contains. As Thomas Goodwin observes, the "prevailing testimony of the Spirit is the ground of all our faith."[7] Without the Spirit, our faith in God's Word would be nothing but crass unbelief.

Without the Word and Spirit, our faith gets lost in a dark maze of gross ignorance. The Word stands as the "basis whereby faith is supported and sustained," says Calvin. "Therefore, take away the Word and no faith will then remain."[8] How can we know that our sins are forgiven if we lack certainty that what God tells us about such absolution is true, namely, that it comes through faith in Christ? God is trustworthy and cannot lie, thus making the truth he reveals the most glorious.

In relation to this truth, theologians have distinguished between implicit and explicit faith in God's Word as the very words (*ipsissima verba*) of God (2 Tim. 3:16). We may implicitly believe that the Word of God and all it contains is true. As finite beings with in-dwelling sin, we remain ignorant of many things in God's Word. As a result, particularly for babes in Christ, we believe many scriptures by implicit faith without knowing the particulars of those passages.

We will strive to move beyond such a state into explicit faith by all the means that God has given to the church.

Explicit faith involves a person believing particular truths. For example, Paul speaks of truths of "first importance": "that Christ died for our sins in accordance with the Scriptures, that he was buried, that he was raised on the third day in accordance with the Scriptures" (1 Cor. 15:3–4). These particular truths must be embraced in their particulars. To be a Christian, then, Paul makes explicit faith a requirement: "If you confess with your mouth that Jesus is Lord and believe in your heart that God raised him from the dead, you will be saved" (Rom. 10:9).

We must believe the Word of God with a supernatural faith because it comes from a source outside ourselves and the created order; it comes from God the Creator of all. What he has stooped down to reveal we believe only because the Spirit has opened our hearts to it. We believe implicitly all that God says and explicitly all that is necessary to be saved. And we do so by the enabling of the Holy Spirit, who lifts us to such heights that we believe what seems impossible. Do not misunderstand what I am saying here; faith lays hold not of something irrational but of truths that we cannot attain in our natural state. Tertullian speaks well when in his work *De carne Christi liber* he writes,

> The Son of God was born: there is no shame, because it is shameful.
> And the Son of God died: it is wholly credible, because it is unsound.
> And, buried, He rose again: it is certain, because impossible [*certum est, quia impossibile*].[9]

Apart from supernatural faith, true belief in Christ's death and resurrection is impossible. But as Tertullian says, "It is certain." Why? Because the Word of God must be believed.

Question 5

Are we justified by believing in the doctrine of justification by faith alone?

No, while faith requires an object, namely,
Christ, we are justified through faith in him,
not in all the details of this doctrine.

The doctrine of justification by faith alone, particularly in the Reformed theological tradition, evolved from the time of the Reformation period.[1] By the seventeenth century, the majority of Reformed theologians accepted the concept of the imputation of Christ's active obedience, though a few prominent theologians dissented. So even in the Reformed tradition, theologians have not agreed on all the details related to the doctrine of justification by faith alone. Thankfully, there exists room for disagreement within limits without placing an orthodox doctrine of salvation in jeopardy.

In connection with this thinking, John Owen says this of justification: "Men may be really saved by that grace which doctrinally they do deny; and they may be justified by the imputation of that righteousness which in opinion they deny to be imputed."[2] A person may truly trust in Christ for forgiveness of sins while being ignorant or in denial of the doctrine of the imputation of Christ's righteousness. Indeed, Owen adds,

> For my part, I had much rather my lot should be found among them who do really believe with the heart unto righteousness, though they are not able to give a tolerable definition of faith unto others, than among them who can endlessly dispute about it with seeming accuracy and skill, but are negligent in the exercise of it as their own duty.[3]

Amen!

If we insist on belief in the fully developed doctrine of justification by faith alone, including the imputation of the righteousness of Christ, then we make faith in correct doctrine, not Christ, the savior. He died even for theological errors. All who will be saved, then, will be saved by the imputation of Christ's righteousness, even if they fail to recognize or acknowledge it. Otherwise, the gates of heaven are a lot narrower than we can imagine (e.g., no classical Arminians or Anabaptists in heaven). Owen also argues,

> For the faith of it is included in that general assent which they give to the truth of the gospel, and such an adherence to Christ may ensue thereon, as that their mistake of the way whereby they are saved by him, shall not defraud them of a real interest therein.[4]

Owen shows that sinners are not justified by believing in particular and debated features of a polished doctrine of justification by faith alone. Rather, sinners are saved through faith alone in Christ alone. Jesus, not a precise formulation of this doctrine, is the object of our faith. Owen adds,

> And for my part, I must say, that notwithstanding all the disputes that I see and read about justification . . . I do not believe

but that the authors of them, (if they be not Socinians) do really trust to the mediation of Christ for the pardon of their sins, and acceptance with God, and not to their own works or obedience. Nor will I believe the contrary, until they expressly declare it.[5]

Here is a generous catholic spirit that might surprise many. Owen draws a line but also shows a great deal of charity toward others, even those outside the Reformed tradition. He understood that a simple trust in Christ for the forgiveness of sins, over against relying on our works of obedience for justification, suffices to enter the kingdom of heaven. This is why the Roman Catholic doctrine of justification is so misleading, because it does its best to keep people from embracing this simple truth.

When you question someone's faith based on an argument that most educated Christians, including many preachers, cannot comprehend, then there is a serious problem. Presbyterians and Reformed folk can go at it over things most of the Christian world cannot even understand.

There is a place to defend this doctrine of justification by faith alone (*sola fide*) from various onslaughts. We must not only understand and protect the teaching but also remember the consequences of the truth for those not embracing it in its fullness. Does not this particular doctrine beget humility and grace in our hearts toward others because of what it means for us? Specifically, it manifests to us that we need a righteousness from Christ that we fail to possess ourselves in our unrighteousness.

Justification through faith alone is glorious precisely because we put our faith in Christ's ability to justify us, not in our knowledge of the Christian religion. Naturally, we aim to be as explicit in our faith as possible, as sound doctrine necessarily strengthens our faith. Still, even those with a simple faith in a great Savior will be saved, provided they look outside themselves to Christ alone to deliver them from their sins.

Question 6

What does our faith lay hold of?

Our faith lays hold of Christ along with
all the saving benefits that are graciously
offered through union with him.

The word *salvation* has a broad semantic range in the New Testament, and does not always refer to how we are justified.[1] It can encompass all our saving benefits, from regeneration to justification to sanctification to glorification (e.g., 1 Tim. 4:16; Heb. 2:3; 1 Pet. 1:9). I believe Reformed theologians have tried to do justice to this New Testament concern, though we should be sensitive to the fact that many American evangelicals have a truncated understanding of the word *salvation*.

Not only justification but also adoption, sanctification, and glorification are gifts given to Christ's people when they receive him by faith. We have the right to all these gifts. But the Christian life is just that: a life. We thus possess eternal life by walking the sanctified life, which includes good works. According to the seventeenth-century Reformed theologian Francis Turretin, good works are required "as the means and way for possessing salvation." Works do not contribute to the acquisition of salvation but "should be considered necessary to the obtainment of it, so that no one can be saved without them." He then goes on to argue,

> This very thing is no less expressly delivered concerning future glory. For since good works have the relation of the means to the end (John 3:5, 16; Mt. 5:8); of the "way" to the goal (Eph. 2:10; Phil. 3:14); of the "sowing" to the harvest (Gal. 6:7, 8); . . . of labor to the reward (Mt. 20:1); of the "contest" to the crown (2 Tim. 2:5; 4:8), everyone sees that there is the highest and an indispensable necessity of good works for obtaining glory. It is so great that it cannot be reached without them (Heb. 12:14; Rev. 21:27).[2]

Good works are the necessary path believers must walk to final salvation. This is in keeping with the Westminster Larger Catechism, which speaks of good works as "the way which [God] has appointed them to salvation" (q. 32). The Westminster Confession of Faith describes "their fruit unto holiness" leading to the end, which likewise reflects the relationship between means and end (16.2).

Similarly, Herman Witsius affirms that the "practice of Christian piety is the way to life, because thereby we go to the possession of the right obtained by Christ." Witsius makes a distinction between the right to (or acquisition of) life and the possession of life. The former is "assigned to the obedience of Christ, that all the value of our holiness may be entirely excluded." However, "our works . . . which the Spirit of Christ works in us, and by us, contribute something to the latter."[3] As George Downame says, "Sanctification, and the duties thereof are not causes of salvation."[4] Good works are not the cause of salvation, but they are the way to salvation—the path on which we walk (Matt. 7:13–14).

So we come to another important distinction (alluded to above) between the "right" and "possession" of salvation. Thomas Goodwin says, "Distinguish between the right and the possession, and you have clearly the Apostle [Paul's] meaning [in Ephesians 2:8–10]."[5] This distinction has several advantages.

First, it helps us to safeguard the fact that when we trust in Christ, we are united to and possess all blessings in him. This denotes the "right" of salvation (based on Christ's meritorious work alone). When we first believe, we are as justified as we will ever be. "Upon believing," says Goodwin, "the whole right of salvation is given us; but all the holiness and works we have do not serve for the right, but only we are led through them to the possession of it."[6]

Second, this distinction helps us to make sense of the "conditional" language of Scripture. For example, consider Philippians 3:12–14:

> Not that I have already obtained this or am already perfect, but I press on to make it my own, because Christ Jesus has made me his own. Brothers, I do not consider that I have made it my own. But one thing I do: forgetting what lies behind and straining forward to what lies ahead, I press on toward the goal for the prize of the upward call of God in Christ Jesus.

Paul knows that he has all spiritual blessings in Christ, yet he speaks of not having obtained final glorification, which causes him to press on to make it his own.

Entering glory comes through a path that God has marked out for his people, one that necessarily involves good works (Eph. 2:8–10). Here, I think, we see one of the many benefits of Reformed scholasticism for present-day debates that have often missed important distinctions and qualifications. As a pastor, I do not like to use big words (such as *eschatological*) in the pulpit or complicate matters for God's people. So how can we make this distinction plain to laypeople?

In this way: Our right to eternal life is based on the imputed righteousness of Christ. Nothing can be added to that, not even a single good work. Justification can never be revoked, an inestimable gift we receive by faith alone. But the final goal of our salvation is our glorification and the blessed vision of Christ (which theologians refer to as the *beatific vision*). When we stand before God, our justification, in which we stand clothed in Christ's perfect righteousness (i.e., his active and passive obedience), enables us to satisfy the demands of God's righteous, holy law.

But we nonetheless have to walk to this destination in order to possess the vision of Christ (eternal life), and the only path to walk is the path of good works. These works have, of course, been prepared in advance for us (Eph. 2:10). Not only must we (i.e., of necessity) walk this way, but also we will (i.e., according to God's promise) walk this way. Christ gifts us with sanctification just as much as he does justification (1 Cor. 1:30), and we can be confident that both will play their appropriate and necessary part in our so great a salvation.

Question 7

Can we lose our justification?

No, we cannot lose our justification, because
it comes by faith alone and because Christ
protects it by his intercession for us.

There are many reasons why God's justification of a sinner cannot be lost or revoked, of which two stand out especially:[1]

1. We are justified by faith alone.
2. Christ intercedes for us.

That sinners are justified by faith alone is a key aspect of the biblical, Reformed doctrine of justification. Interestingly, Martin Luther may never have called justification "the article by which the church stands or falls" (*articulus stantis aut cadentis Ecclesiae*), even though the concept is clearly found in his writings.[2]

The phrase "by faith alone" (*sola fide*) originated with Luther, though the idea is much older. In his German translation of Romans 3:28, Luther added the word *allein* ("alone"), rendering "justified by faith" as "justified by faith alone." John Owen speaks of and defends justification by faith alone by noting,

It is faith alone which on our part is required to interest us in that righteousness, or whereby we comply with God's grant and communication of it, or receive it unto our use and benefit; for although this faith is in itself the radical principle of all obedience, . . . yet, as we are justified by it, its act and duty is such, or of that nature, as that no other grace, duty, or work, can be associated with it, or be of any consideration.[3]

Owen offers a fivefold argument for "faith alone."

First, the New Testament speaks of justifying faith most frequently as "receiving." Only faith can accept Christ, "and what it receives is the cause of our justification" (cf. John 1:12). Moreover, we receive even the grace of God and righteousness itself, which are, respectively, "the efficient and material cause of our justification."[4]

Second, "faith is expressed by looking" on Christ alone (cf. John 3:14–15). In this looking, "the nature of faith is expressed," and faith is therefore "exclusive of all other graces and duties whatever."[5]

Third, faith denotes coming to Christ (Matt. 11:28). "To come unto Christ for life and salvation," Owen explains, "is to believe on him unto the justification of life; but no other grace or duty is a coming unto Christ: and therefore have they no place in justification."[6]

Fourth, faith is expressed by "fleeing for refuge" (cf. Heb. 6:18):

For herein it is supposed that he who believes is antecedently thereunto convinced of his lost condition, and that if he abide therein he must perish eternally; that he has nothing of himself whereby he may be delivered from it; that he must betake himself unto somewhat else for relief; that unto this end he considers Christ as set before him, and proposed unto him in the promise of the gospel; that he judges this to be a holy, a safe way, for his deliverance and acceptance with God.[7]

Fifth, the terms by which the Old Testament expresses faith, as Owen describes them, are "leaning on God . . . or Christ," "resting on God," "cleaving unto the Lord," and also "trusting, hoping, and waiting." Those who act on this type of faith "declare themselves to be lost, hopeless, helpless, desolate, poor, orphans; whereon they place all their hope and expectation on God alone."[8]

Knowing that the Scriptures do not explicitly say, "Justification is by faith alone," Owen maintains that the words "by faith in his blood" imply the doctrine. For "faith respecting the blood of Christ" is that by which "propitiation was made for sin," and such faith "admits of no association with any other graces or duties."[9]

The doctrine of justification by faith alone finds its roots firmly in the Scriptures. But the teaching itself requires not a proof text here and there but verification "by good and necessary consequence" (WCF 1.6). Some may be sheepish about proving infant baptism according to good and necessary consequence (cf. Matt. 22:32), but this principle of interpretation is vital to the "alone" in how we are justified.

If we were not justified by faith alone, then some other "qualification" would bring our state of justification into doubt, since we would have to do something other than simply receive Christ. If justification is not at once complete but rather in need of a second justification, "no man can be justified in this world."[10]

The second reason we can never lose our justification is because of Christ's intercession. The application of both the life and death of Christ relate to his intercession. Distinguishing the two concepts, Reformed theologians such as Thomas Goodwin call his death "the means of procurement or obtaining it for us; but his intercession . . . the means of applying all unto us."[11]

Therefore, the justification of the ungodly depends on Christ's intercession. In fact, the continuation of our justification depends on his ongoing intercession, by which he renews the merits of his death for his sheep every moment in heaven before the Father.

Goodwin adds, "We owe our standing in grace every moment to his sitting in heaven and interceding every moment."[12]

This means that Christ would have to relinquish his office as priest in order for someone to lose his or her justification. Jesus would have to neglect or forget about his people. So, pastorally speaking, we can say, "You can lose your justification when Christ decides he no longer wants to be High Priest." Or more provocatively, "You will lose your justification when Christ decides he no longer wants to be merciful." Since the Spirit dwells in Christ to the fullest measure possible, we can be sure that he will not forget us or become unmerciful toward us.

Christ is infinitely more interested in maintaining the justification of his people than they can ever be. The Father is also adamant that his Son should fulfill his office of High Priest for his people. If God is for us, who can be against us? Not Christ—that much is sure. After all, the Father has made a declaration, and Christ wants to honor his Father's declaration by fulfilling his call to be a faithful and sympathetic High Priest.

Question 8

Is faith our righteousness?

No, faith is the sole instrument whereby God
graciously imputes to us the righteousness of Christ.

According to B. B. Warfield in his masterful work "The Biblical
Doctrine of Faith," "the place of faith in the process of salvation,
as biblically conceived, could scarcely . . . be better described than
by the use of the scholastic term 'instrumental cause.'"[1] Faith is an
instrument whereby we receive justification from God. It is not a
"work" in the sense that it equals or is counted for our righteousness before God.[2]

Historically, according to the judgment of many Reformed divines, Jacob Arminius and his Remonstrant (Arminian) successors
deviated from the Reformed doctrine of justification by faith alone
in a significant way. As in other doctrines, Arminius and his followers seem to hold to a view that is more Socinian and Roman
Catholic than Reformed. While recognizing some such differences,
Michael Horton nonetheless argues that "the classical Arminianism
of the original Remonstrants (led by Arminius) affirmed justification through faith alone."[3] However, as I hope to show below, the

Arminian (Remonstrant) departs somewhat from the Reformed view on justification.

Franciscus Gomarus, the famous opponent of Arminius, maintained that "not the doctrine of predestination but that of justification" became the "cardinal point on which Arminius deviated from Reformed doctrine."[4] Gomarus fought with Arminius over this doctrine not because of irrelevant differences. Herman Witsius also drew attention to this aberration: "Arminius, by his subtlety, frames vain empty quibbles, when he contends that the righteousness of Christ cannot be imputed to us for righteousness." Witsius added, "It is well known that the reformed churches condemned Arminius and his followers, for saying that faith comes to be considered in the matter of justification as a work or act of ours."[5]

But what is this unorthodox view as put forward by Arminius and some of his followers? For Arminius, because of the gracious estimation of God, he credits our faith as our righteousness. The righteousness of Christ is not imputed to believers, according to at least the later Arminius.[6] He did not believe Christ's righteousness could be imputed. In discussing justification, Arminius made use of the Latin term *acceptilatio*, which means a "formal release from an obligation." Imperfect faith, then, is accepted by God's gracious estimation as righteousness. Or to put it another way, the human act of faith is by grace counted as evangelical righteousness, *as if* it were the complete fulfillment of the whole law, even though it is not. This genuine human act comes forth from the ability to choose.

What is the problem? Because the act of faith constitutes righteousness, God declares a sinner justified not because of Christ's imputed righteousness received by faith but because of faith counted as righteousness. The ground of justification is my faith, not Christ's righteousness. However, as Bavinck correctly argues, "Faith never occurs as righteousness itself or as a part of it. . . . Faith does not justify by its own essence or act because itself is righteousness, but by its content, because it is faith in Christ, who is our righteousness."[7] Indeed, what would be the point of Christ as the object of faith if faith itself were our righteousness?

From the Arminian Petrus Bertius we might conclude that the Reformed and Remonstrants seemed to agree on imputation as the formal cause (i.e., structure) of justification but differed on the material cause (i.e., what is actually imputed). What is imputed to the believer, our act of faith or Christ's righteousness apprehended by faith? The Reformed held to the latter, whereas, as noted above, the Arminians typically held to the former. But even on the so-called formal cause there was an important difference between the two camps. Based on what I have said above, imputation for the Arminians is an *aestimatio* ("estimation")—God considers our righteousness (i.e., faith) as something that it is not (i.e., perfect). The Reformed, however, view imputation as *secundum veritatem* ("according to truth")—God considers Christ's righteousness as ours, precisely because it is ours, through union with him. The verdict that God passes on his Son is precisely the same as that which he passes on those who belong to him—"righteous"—but only through imputation.

The Roman Catholic and Arminian treatments of the act of faith seem to reveal a similarity between the two positions. But for the Roman Catholics, faith is only the beginning of justification, whereas for an Arminian such as Bertius, faith is the perfect righteousness of the law. Sibrandus Lubbertus, a Reformed opponent of Bertius and the Arminians, makes the following point concerning Bertius:

> For although the Papists teach that we are justified by faith taken in the literal sense, yet they do not teach that faith is our whole righteousness: they just teach that faith is the beginning of our justification. . . . Servetus, however, and Socinus teach that faith is our whole righteousness, as has been shown

before, and they reject [Christ's] merit. So because you say that we are justified by faith, taken in the literal sense, and in contrast deny, against the Papists, that faith is only the beginning of our justification, and [because you] add from Servetus and Socinus that it is the perfect fulfillment of the law, that is, it is the whole and perfect righteousness by which we are justified before God; because you finally deny against the Papists the merit of faith, and assert, with Servetus and Socinus, that it justifies because of God's valuation, [therefore] everybody sees that you come closer to Servetus and Socinus than to the Papists and for that reason it can be more correctly said that you are disciples of Servetus and Socinus than those of the Papists.[8]

In Socinus's view, God considers faith our righteousness. Thus, Roman Catholics, Arminians, and Socinians all reject the notion that Christ's righteousness is imputed to the believer.

In summary, no uniform doctrine of justification exists in Christendom. The Reformed theologian William Perkins highlights the importance of the Reformed view on imputation:

> For as his righteousness is made ours, so are his merits depending thereon: but his righteousness is made ours by imputation. . . . Hence arises another point, namely, that as Christ's righteousness is made ours really by imputation to make us righteous: so we by the merit of his righteousness imputed do merit and deserve life everlasting. And this is our doctrine.[9]

This is our Reformed doctrine. Justification by faith alone is simply that. And the gift of faith is the instrument that receives the merits of Christ.

We can have the greatest confidence, then, that at the final judgment we shall enter glory. Why? Because we really possess Christ's righteousness. God will not—indeed, cannot—deny what is rightfully ours through Christ Jesus.

To put it another way: God could bar us from heaven only if he were prepared to excommunicate his own Son from heaven. As safe as Christ is in heaven, so are his people. Faith, then, is the gracious gift that enables us to have such confidence in Christ.

Question 9

What is the principal exercise of faith?

The contemplation of the glory of Christ
is the principal exercise of faith.

John Owen referred to the contemplation of the glory of Christ as "the principal exercise of faith."[1] This magnificent statement finds its foundation in an equally glorious truth: those wishing to behold the glory of God in Christ in the coming life must behold the same in this life by faith. For "we walk by faith, not by sight" (2 Cor. 5:7). We cannot adequately understand the life of faith until we face the reality that our lives consist in "beholding the glory of the Lord" by faith; in so doing, we are "transformed into the same image [of Christ] from one degree of glory to another" (2 Cor. 3:18).

Satan blinds unbelievers to seeing the glory of God in Christ. Conversely, the Spirit gives us an "unveiled face" (2 Cor. 3:18) in order to perceive such glory in the gospel. This sight does not occur as a one-time event or even as a future hope but as a daily reality gripping our souls to consider why and how we live. As Owen laments, most Christians are "strangers unto this duty."[2]

Most Christians today are not merely ignorant of essential truths of Christ's person and work but grossly so. Solid, intense, soul-devoting study of Christ remains absent from the lives of many Christians today. Churches fail to proclaim the unsearchable riches of Christ, the visible image of the invisible God (Col. 1:15), as they should. The result? God's people neglect the principal exercise of faith: contemplation of Christ's glory. So in Owen's most fitting estimation,

> Did we abound in this duty, in this exercise of faith, our life in walking before God would be more sweet and pleasant unto us—our spiritual light and strength would have a daily increase; —we should more represent the glory of Christ in our ways and walking than usually we do, and death itself would be most welcome unto us.[3]

That last sentence gets to the heart of the issue. Why are so many people, even Christians, afraid of death? Because we have not, in the exercise of our faith, sufficiently grasped the glory of Christ that awaits his people. In some of the most splendid words ever uttered in the history of the world, Christ prayed, "Father, I desire that they also, whom you have given me, may be with me where I am, to see my glory that you have given me because you loved me before the foundation of the world" (John 17:24). He prayed these words to help us deal with death but also to give us a "positive" look at death: the full contemplation of his glory in his presence, of which we begin to taste now on earth.

Christ desires that we see his glory, but we so often do not share the same wishes. God shines into our hearts the "light of the knowledge of the glory of God in the face of Jesus Christ" (2 Cor. 4:6). That is, God has bestowed on us this unique dignity, but perhaps we fail to understand how blessed we are. As a result, we fail to make the most of this blessing.

Think of the things to which you give attention. How do you exercise your mind? In the contemplation of money, possessions, friends, and prestige? With what are you obsessed? Work, sports, music, politics, Xbox, or Facebook? This may sound shocking, but only those who contemplate Christ's glory will one day see his glory. Why? Because true faith can have no other end (or goal) than being with him as the object of our faith. Our faith is not ignorant of itself. We look to Christ, not to our faith. In looking to him, we live in contemplation of him as we long to be with him. The prospect of seeing Christ, in his peculiar glory as the God-man, should ravish our hearts with an anticipation that fills us with daily delights.

We know and love God's attributes in and through Christ. Therefore, to know God, we must know Christ. The contemplation of Christ brings us to the contemplation of God. God's wisdom, power, justice, goodness, mercy, faithfulness, and patience are nowhere better displayed than in the life, death, resurrection, ascension, and enthronement of Jesus. So when we contemplate these aspects of Christ's work, we come to love the holy properties of our great God. God and Christ are the objects of our faith: "Truly, truly, I say to you, whoever hears my word and believes him who sent me has eternal life. He does not come into judgment, but has passed from death to life" (John 5:24). Faith in Christ necessarily brings us to God, and faith in God necessarily brings us back to Christ. As a result, Thomas Watson calls faith an "assimilating" or conforming grace. Why?

> [Because] it changes the soul into the image of the object; it makes it like Christ. Never did any look upon Christ with a believing eye, but he was made like Christ. A deformed person may look on a beautiful object, and not be made beautiful; but faith looking on Christ transforms a man, and turns him into his similitude. Looking on a bleeding Christ causes a soft bleed-

ing heart; looking on a holy Christ causes sanctity of heart; looking on a humble Christ makes the soul humble. As the chameleon is changed into the colour of that which it looks upon, so faith, looking on Christ, changes the Christian into the similitude of Christ.[4]

Beautiful. No wonder John Owen said the principal exercise of saving faith is to behold Christ in his person and work.

Question 10

What is the principle of our obedience?

Faith, by which we are sanctified,
is the principle of our obedience.

Whatever does not come from faith is sin. So sanctification always involves faith. When Paul speaks of his conversion, he notes that he was called to preach to the Gentiles and "open their eyes, so that they may turn from darkness to light and from the power of Satan to God, that they may receive forgiveness of sins and a place among *those who are sanctified by faith in me*" (Acts 26:18).

We may with Thomas Watson call faith a "refining grace." In the soul, faith acts as a "fire among metals; it refines and purifies." He adds, "Morality may wash the outside, faith washes the inside. 'Having purified their hearts by faith' (Acts 15:9). . . . Faith is a virgin-grace: though it does not take away the life of sin, yet it takes away the love of sin."[1]

We find the greatest Old Testament example of faith in Abraham (without denying his place in redemptive history) in Genesis 22. Few stories are more moving, harrowing, dramatic, or delightful than the story of Abraham going to the mount to sacrifice his only legitimate son, Isaac, at the command of God. Even at Abraham's late age, God was sanctifying him. Faith stood as the principle by which he obeyed God.

God never meant the Christian life to be complicated, and he never deceives or confuses us. His demands are actually rather straightforward, as the Preacher says at the end of Ecclesiastes: "The end of the matter; all has been heard. Fear God and keep his commandments, for this is the whole duty of man. For God will bring every deed into judgment, with every secret thing, whether good or evil" (Eccles. 12:13–14). We are the ones who make the Christian life problematic and complex, not God. The "secret" of the true spiritual life is always simple: will you trust and obey God?

In Genesis 22, "son" (used ten times) emerges as the key term in the narrative. God brought the trial years after Abraham had experienced perhaps his greatest joy, the birth of his son Isaac. God then tested Abraham, not to do something wrong but to see whether he proved worthy. God wanted not Isaac's death but Abraham's trust.

God drove home to Abraham what he already knew, namely, that he greatly loved his son (Gen. 22:1–2). Abraham responded in faith (Gen. 22:3). He had already manifested a love for God greater than that for his father, Terah (Genesis 12). But now Abraham had to show that his love for God was greater than that for his son Isaac, a far more excruciating test of faith. The trial remains deeply mysterious. Must the father of the faithful (cf. Gen. 17:5; Rom. 4:17) be the monster of all fathers?

Abraham's faith explains his immediate response of obedience (Gen. 22:3, "rose early in the morning"). When John Eck questioned Martin Luther at the Diet of Worms (April 16, 1521), especially whether he would retract the doctrines in his books, Luther asked for more time to respond. We can certainly appreciate his reluctance, but Abraham showed none. Likewise, he did not try to find and substitute Ishmael as a sacrifice. Finally, he refused to debate with God as he had done in the cases of Ishmael and Lot. He simply obeyed.

By faith he placed the most precious thing in the world to him on the altar. Perhaps verse 5 represents words of such great faith that no person that side of Christ's death and resurrection could fully appreciate. Abraham told his servants that he and Isaac were going to worship and would return again. In other words, he believed that somehow he would return with Isaac. The author of Hebrews highlights this confidence explicitly:

> By faith Abraham, when he was tested, offered up Isaac, and he who had received the promises was in the act of offering up his only son, of whom it was said, "Through Isaac shall your offspring be named." He considered that God was able even to raise him from the dead, from which, figuratively speaking, he did receive him back. (Heb. 11:17–19)

Abraham trusted that God would give back Isaac from the dead, long before God had raised Jesus (or anyone that we know of, for that matter) from the dead. Abraham's faith was hope in God's resurrection power. As Isaac carried the wood for his own destruction, Abraham must have been filled with all sorts of emotional struggles. But his faith ultimately won over his emotions as he placed his son on the altar and raised his hand to kill him.

They say there's a word for the loss of a spouse or a parent but not for that of a child, which seems so unnatural. What Abraham was about to do was so abnormal, yet his supernatural faith made him prefer trusting and obeying God to satisfying the desires of his flesh. After all, Abraham had plenty of experience with the latter concerning his wife, Sarah, whom he allowed to be possibly defiled because he did not trust God but rather sought to protect himself.

The Lord intervened at the best possible time, for his timing is always perfect (Gen. 22:11–13). We forget what it was like for the angel of the Lord to intervene. It meant that he would replace Isaac as the true sacrifice. It meant that when the angel of the Lord, the Lord Jesus Christ, was crucified, no such angel would keep him from dying on the cross. As the angel told Abraham not to lay a hand on the boy, Abraham's faith was fully vindicated. Abraham trusted God and kept nothing back in so doing. Thus, his faith was not merely assent to God's command but an unwavering trust that God would do what is right (see Gen. 18:25, "Shall not the Judge of all the earth do what is just?").

John Ball rightly observes, "To live by faith is firmly to rely upon the Word of God in all estates and conditions, with full purpose to be guided by it, until the good things contained therein be fully accomplished."[2] Abraham firmly relied on the word of God in the most difficult of circumstances and was guided by God's command, word, and promise. He saw good things accomplished, namely, the receiving back of his son from the dead (Heb. 11:19). But all of this happened because he lived by faith. Without faith, it is impossible either to obey or to please God. Abraham did both. Concerning the connection between the faith and obedience of the patriarchs, Warfield notes,

> This does not mean, of course, that with them faith took the place of obedience: an entire self-commitment to God which did not show itself in obedience to Him would be self-contradictory, and the testing of faith by obedience is therefore a marked feature of the patriarchal narrative. But it does mean that faith was with them the precondition of all obedience. The patriarchal religion is essentially a religion, not of law but of promise, and therefore not primarily of obedience but of trust.[3]

Faith lies behind Abraham's obedience and, indeed, behind that of all God's servants. Faith exists as the most basic presupposition of obedience. Without the former, the latter cannot be; it becomes impossible to please God. Let us make no mistake here: Abraham was a better (more Christlike) man after this trial than before. Not only was his faith vindicated, but also in the process of this trial, he experienced more of God's mercy and love than ever before. As a result, Abraham expressed greater love for God than ever before.

In the end, Abraham's whole life was delivered down to us as an example of what it means to live by faith. Abraham was an obedient servant who yearned for his heavenly call because he was a man of faith. Our whole lives must be ordered by faith if we are to be obedient to God's calling. God's calling, as we see from Scripture, is sometimes so difficult that obedience to such would be impossible apart from faith in God.

In addition to being the object of our faith, is Jesus also the pattern of our faith?

This we happily affirm, for Jesus is the greatest example of believing ever.

Jesus lived by faith.[1] We live by faith. As Thomas Goodwin says, Jesus "was put to live by faith [just] as we are."[2] Herman Bavinck correctly notes that Reformed theologians, against the Roman Catholics, "maintained that as a human being on earth Christ had lived by faith."[3]

Jesus had a faith for justification: "He who vindicates [i.e., justifies] me is near" (Isa. 50:8). He believed that God would justify/vindicate him, which God did at the resurrection (1 Tim. 3:16). We also have a faith for justification: "And to the one who does not work but believes in him who justifies the ungodly . . ." (Rom. 4:5).

However, Jesus did not look to a mediator as the object of his faith. He looked to God to justify him for his own obedience. Unlike us, he placed his faith not in the mercy of God toward him but in the righteousness of God toward him (Ps. 16:8–10; Acts 2:25–27). For us, both God and Christ are the objects of our faith (John 14:1). We must not look to our own obedience for justification, as Christ did. Rather, we must look to his obedience for our justification. Our faith is in God's mercy in Christ (see WCF 14.2, which speaks of the "principal acts of saving faith").

But what about Jesus as our example or pattern of believing? Should we try to imitate him? Of course. The Scriptures are clear on this matter: "Be imitators of me," Paul says, "as I am of Christ" (1 Cor. 11:1). Even though the church in its history has sometimes insufficiently emphasized "Christ for us," that does not mean that we can discard the plain teaching of Scripture that Christ is our example. We do not need to neglect asking, "What would Jesus do?" just because theological liberals have distorted this question.[4]

Goodwin says that in the example of Christ's faith, "we have the highest instance of believing that ever was."[5] In other words, this Westminster divine calls Jesus the greatest believer who ever lived. Jesus trusted God's promises to him, even in the midst of suffering, which in the end he knew was the only way to glory. Should we not imitate Jesus in this manner? Goodwin adds,

> This example of Christ may teach and incite us to believe. For did Christ lay down all his glory, and empty himself, and leave himself worth nothing, but made a deed of surrendering all he had into his Father's hands, and this in a pure trust that God would "justify many by him"? And shall not we lay down all we have, and part with whatever is dear unto us aforehand, with the like submission, in a dependence and hope of being ourselves justified by him?[6]

Viewing Christ as both the object and the pattern of our faith is not to see two enemies but to see two friends (Phil. 2:5–11). This is why John Owen, commenting on Hebrews 2:13, says,

> It was [Christ's] duty no less than it is theirs to depend on God in troubles and distresses. . . . And as such his duty it was, in all straits, to betake himself by faith unto the care and protection of God. . . . There was upon [Jesus] a confluence of every thing that is evil or troublesome unto human nature. And herein is he principally our example, at least so far that we should think no kind of suffering strange unto us. . . . [Jesus] is a precedent unto us in trusting as well as in suffering.[7]

John Calvin likewise affirms not only that Christ trusted God but also that we can be encouraged in the way we look to Christ as our "leader":

> As then [Jesus] depended on God's aid, his lot is the same with ours. It is surely not in vain or for nothing that we trust in God; for were we destitute of his grace, we should be miserable and lost. The trust then which we put in God, is an evidence of our helplessness. At the same time we differ from Christ in this—the weakness which necessarily and naturally belongs to us he willingly undertook. But it ought not a little to encourage us to trust in God, that we have Christ as our leader and instructor; for who would fear to go astray while following in his steps?[8]

Jesus had to live by faith for without faith it is impossible to please God (Heb. 11:6). His vicarious obedience on our behalf would not have been acceptable or pleasing to God if it did not proceed from a principle of faith. Jesus had to live by faith because he is the pioneer and perfecter of our faith (Heb. 12:2). Christ did not exercise faith merely for himself; he also exercised faith for all those for whom he died, so that they might receive from him that particular grace. For there is no grace we accept—whether faith, justification, sanctification, adoption, or glorification—that was not first present in Christ himself, particularly the grace of faith.

As Richard Sibbes notes, "We must know that all things are first in Christ, and then in us."[9]

Jesus had to live the perfect life of faith because our lives of faith are so utterly imperfect (Mark 9:24). But that does not mean, of course, that we should not desire to emulate him in the way he trusted his Father to make good on all the promises that were rightly his. As Bavinck says, "Faith for . . . Christ was nothing other than the act of clinging to the word and promises of God."[10] Should we not do likewise, that is, cling to the promises of God, which are "Yes" and "Amen" in Christ Jesus (2 Cor. 1:20)? After all, Owen notes, Jesus "is in the eye of God as the idea of what he intends in us, in the communication of grace and glory; and he ought to be so in ours, as unto all that we aim at in a way of duty."[11]

Did Christ know that all things were working together for his good when he was arrested in the garden? Yes. How? He embraced that truth by faith. We must do likewise when we are in our "gardens of despair" (cf. Ps. 22:9–11; Rom. 8:28).

If even his enemies acknowledged that Jesus trusted in God (Matt. 27:43), then surely his friends must too. Jesus believed that he would be in paradise after dying on the cross. "Christ knew very well," observes Geerhardus Vos, "why He was abandoned in this hour and had perfect faith and confidence in His Father."[12] Praise God that Jesus was both the object and pattern of the dying thief's faith (Luke 23:43), and that he is so for all those who wish to live like their Master: in unwavering trust in God and his promises.

Question 12

Can faith be increased
and strengthened?

Yes, faith may be increased and strengthened by the
Spirit through the Word, sacraments, and prayer.

Faith has degrees. Some possess "weak" and others "strong" faith
(Rom. 14:1–15:7).[1] In Romans 14, the theology of the weak will
not allow them to eat foods that are acceptable. Their faith will
become "stronger" when they learn better what God allows for
and requires of them. In other contexts, Christians have trouble
believing God's promises to them.

Faith exists as the antithesis of anxiety (Matt. 6:30–31), fear
(Mark 4:40), and doubt (Matt. 21:21). Yet Christians with faith
still experience this trio of life struggles. Such difficulties do not
nullify their faith but do highlight the weakness of it. God does not
tell us to pick ourselves up by our bootstraps if we desire greater
faith. Rather, he gives means to nurture faith, namely, the Word of
God, the administration of the sacraments, and prayer.

True and accurate knowledge of the Scriptures, when accompanied by the powerful working of the Holy Spirit, strengthens our faith. The more we understand God's promises in his Word and his gracious purposes toward us in Christ, the more we are assured in our faith. Such faith fortifies itself with the Word of God. "Faith needs the Word," says John Calvin, "as much as fruit needs the living root of a tree."[2] As our faith becomes more and more "explicit" (as seen in chap. 4: faith in the particulars of our salvation), we are due to be stronger in our trust.

I remember when I first read Thomas Goodwin's *The Heart of Christ in Heaven towards Sinners on Earth*, which greatly strengthened my faith in God.[3] Goodwin increased my awareness, more clearly than ever, of Christ's resolve to save me. Assured of Christ's desire to be with me, based on the teaching of God's Word (John 17:24), I was more excited and desirous (and better prepared) to be with Christ. Love casts out fear, and understanding the love of Christ toward sinners on earth drives us to that end.

As a pastor, then, I must point the people of God to the great truths of Scripture each Lord's Day. When I preach the Word of God, his people, who listen by faith, are strengthened in faith. This is because God appointed faithful preaching as a means of sanctifying his people. And this is why, in worship, we should read, preach, sing, and pray the Word. In the church today, too often God's words are removed and replaced by man's. Tragic.

The crisis of assurance afflicting so many of God's people can be cured by his truth. In addition to his spoken word, he gave the sacraments (baptism and the Lord's Supper) as the "visible word." That spoken to the ear in the Word is presented to the eyes in the sacraments, passing through the senses to our hearts, minds, and souls. God ordained these sacraments to strengthen our faith.

The sacraments contain promises, which according to John Ball, are "firm grounds" whereby the faithful soul, making use of the Word and sacraments, "shall be made wise unto salvation, confirmed in faith, strengthened in grace, refreshed with joy and comfort, and perfected unto everlasting happiness."[4] Those who do not diligently approach public worship in faith, with "reverence and awe" (Heb. 12:28), are emaciated Christians, refusing to open their mouths for God to feed them.

God appointed prayer as a third means to strengthen faith. Yet speaking to God in prayer requires faith (Heb. 11:6). Sometimes we stumble to him, hesitating, barely making it to the throne of grace, as though hobbling after sustaining a horrific injury. It seems as though nothing in the Christian life comes so difficult as prayer. By the way, the Devil knows this all too well. He will do all that he can to keep us from prayer and so away from God and the other means he uses for our sanctification.

There is no explicit rule set down in Scripture for how often and how long we should pray. Yet we are to pray "without ceasing" (1 Thess. 5:17), "at all times" (Eph. 6:18), and suddenly, based on the need and occasion (Neh. 2:4). These actions all indicate how essential it is for believers to maintain an ever-ready prayerful spirit in the Christian life.

The Bible also gives us examples of those who devoted themselves to prayer at set times (Matt. 6:6). Consider Daniel, who, even when it was illegal to pray to God at all, openly prayed three times daily, "as he had done previously" (Dan. 6:10). Little wonder, then, that Daniel had such great faith!

Given that prayer is so difficult, how does Christ motivate us to pray? In Matthew 6:6, he promises his disciples that their Father will reward them for what they do (i.e., pray) in secret. Notice how often the word "reward" appears in that chapter alone. Do we really believe this promise, as we should, that God will reward us for our prayers (though not because we deserve it)? If we did, we would indeed spend a lot more time crying out to God. We do not have, because we do not ask (James 4:2)! We do not ask because we lack faith (Matt. 21:22). Faith is the hand that begs from God: "And without faith it is impossible to please him, for whoever would draw near to God must believe that he exists and that he rewards those who seek him" (Heb. 11:6).

Christ, the man of faith par excellence, certainly grasped this concept in his own prayer life. In fact, he prayed for his reward: "And now, Father, glorify me in your own presence with the glory that I had with you before the world existed" (John 17:5).

God gives and gives. The Father spoke for our benefit. For the same, the Son lived, died, and rose again. And the Spirit dwells in us. The Word, sacraments, and prayer are all means appointed by God and given from his hand so that we may grow in our faith.

Question 13

Should those with saving faith fear God and tremble at his threats?

Yes, those with saving faith should
possess a filial fear and trembling that
reveres God as Father and keeps them
from a servile terror of him as Judge.

In the Westminster Confession of Faith, the divines argue that "the principal acts of saving faith are accepting, receiving, and resting upon Christ alone for justification, sanctification, and eternal life, by virtue of the covenant of grace" (14.2).[1] Before the divines wrote this, William Ames had noted,

> Faith is not wholly concerned about God's threatenings in themselves, because they do not make available the good for us to receive; nor about God's commandments in themselves, because they declare the good to be done, not to be received. . . . But faith is rooted in the promises, because in them is set forth a good to be embraced. Therefore, our theologians are accustomed to make the promises the primary object of faith.[2]

However, that teaching does not exclude the place for the fear of God and the fear of his judgments. One involves the filial fear we are to have toward a holy God who is our Father; the other involves a fear when we have willfully placed ourselves in a position to be judged by him with dire consequences. The Westminster Confession of Faith states that saving faith believes

> whatsoever is revealed in the Word . . . and acts differently upon that which each particular passage thereof contains; yielding obedience to the commands, trembling at the threatenings, and embracing the promises of God for this life, and that which is to come. (14.2)

Faith not only embraces promises (principally) but also trembles at threats (secondarily). This trembling occurs when reasons exist to do so.

Fear is an ordinary part of the Christian life. Consider the psalmist:

> The angel of the LORD encamps
> around those who fear him, and delivers them.
>
> Oh, taste and see that the LORD is good!
> Blessed is the man who takes refuge in him!
> Oh, fear the LORD, you his saints,
> for those who fear him have no lack!
> The young lions suffer want and hunger;
> but those who seek the LORD lack no good thing.
>
> Come, O children, listen to me;
> I will teach you the fear of the LORD. (Ps. 34:7–11)

We are to "serve the LORD with fear, and rejoice with trembling" (Ps. 2:11).

Now the life of faith does not mean that the godly person slavishly fears falling into apostasy. But there are temporal and eternal threats in God's Word applied to the visible church. Denying this concept puts our theology before that revealed by God.

God, as Adam's Father, threatened him in the garden. This threat was an act of love designed to keep Adam from sinning. He had good reason, then, to be afraid of God when he sinned, since he could still recollect God's recent threat concerning the consequences of rebellion. Adam's first sin was unbelief, but he also clearly forgot to fear God in terms of the filial fear he should have had before he had fallen. Adam thus failed in the filial fear of faith, and that led to a servile fear of unbelief, which manifested itself when he hid.

Adam failed to take both God's loving promises and threatenings seriously. Thus, the Lord knows how to keep us living in the fear of him. His promises prompt us to serve him freely and willingly, and his threatenings prevent us from living in carnal presumption on his grace.

Some of the most terrifying threats in Scripture are made to God's people. Are they rightly called "gospel threatenings," as many Reformed divines have suggested? The Canons of Dort shed some light on this question. The fifth head of doctrine ("Of the Perseverance of the Saints"), article 14, is perhaps the most relevant section. Based on the official French edition of the Canons (there is no "official" English version), article 14 reads,

> And as it has pleased God to begin in us by his grace, this his work by the preaching of the gospel: just so he confirms it, maintains and fulfills it by the hearing, reading, meditation, exhortation, threats, and promises of the same gospel, as also by the use of the sacraments.[3]

Clearly, the threats come by "the same gospel" (*du mesme Evangile*) as the promises.

The New Testament issues many threats to the visible people of

God, warning them if they persist in a certain path of unrighteousness (e.g., Matt. 6:15; Mark 1:14–15; Rom. 8:13; 1 Cor. 10:1–22; Gal. 5:21; Heb. 10:25–31; 12:15–17; the whole tenor of Hebrews; Rev. 3:14–22). Moreover, church discipline shows clearly that professing believers can be threatened and even handed over to Satan if they fail to repent. It must be a "gospel threat" because the sin is directly against Christ and his work.

In the *Synopsis of Purer Theology* (*Synopsis Purioris Theologiae*), the authors say, "The gospel contains its own commands, promises, and warnings."[4] Here the *Synopsis* is in agreement with the Canons of Dort and the Westminster Confession of Faith.

In short, sometimes pastors need to strongly warn professing believers when they indulge in sin, because they may be deceiving themselves that they are on a path to heaven when they are really on a path to hell. Paul warned the Corinthians when they acted wickedly (1 Cor. 10:1–22), and Christ did the same for the Laodiceans (Rev. 3:14–22). We must warn God's people when there exists a biblical reason to warn them. Our warnings do not mean that we jettison the indicatives of the gospel. However, the neglect of these very indicatives gives cause to fear the judgments of God (Heb. 2:1–3). According to John Owen, "Every threatening of the gospel proclaims the grace of Christ" to the souls of Christians.[5] He adds, "Man threatens me if I forsake not the gospel; but God threatens me if I do."[6] "How shall we escape if we neglect such a great salvation?" (Heb. 2:3).

John Murray crystalizes perfectly how we must speak of the fear of God and the fear of God's judgments:

> The fear of God which is the soul of godliness does not consist . . . in the dread which is produced by the apprehension of God's wrath. When the reason for such dread exists, then to be destitute of it is the sign of hardened ungodliness. But the fear of God which is the basis of godliness, and in which godliness

may be said to consist, is much more inclusive and determinative than the fear of God's judgment. And we must remember that the dread of judgment will never of itself generate within us the love of God or hatred of the sin that makes us liable to his wrath. Even the infliction of wrath will not create the hatred of sin; it will incite to greater love of sin and enmity against God. Punishment has of itself no regenerating or converting power. The fear of God in which godliness consists is the fear which constrains adoration and love. It is the fear which consists in awe, reverence, honour, and worship, and all of these on the highest level of exercise. It is the reflex in our consciousness of the transcendent majesty and holiness of God. It belongs to all created rational beings and does not take its origins from sin.[7]

Murray makes several important points here. He rightly notes that if a professing Christian has a reason to be afraid of God (e.g., he or she willingly forsakes the assembling of believers, Heb. 10:25–31), then it would be impious not to be fearful. However, the constant godly fear that consists in awe and constrains love keeps a person from certain sins that place him or her more directly under God's judgments. In other words, the fear (reverence) of God keeps us from having to fear the judgments of God. All this is to say, saving faith responds to the God of the Bible, not the god of our imaginations. Our faith necessarily leads to the godly fear of God.

Question 14

Is there such a thing as false faith?

Yes, many possess false faith, faith that
may appear real but is not supernatural.

The Bible makes clear that many "believe" but do not possess true, saving faith. They appear to have faith because they confess their faith, but their faith lacks a supernatural root, which comes from God alone. Christ's ministry offers several examples of this sad reality. In John 2:23, for example, we are told, "Many believed in his name when they saw the signs that he was doing." At face value, this seems wonderful, until we learn that they did not possess genuine faith. John 2:23–24 contains a wordplay; we learn that some had faith (*pisteuō*) in Christ (v. 23) but that "Jesus on his part did not entrust [*episteuen*] himself to them, because he knew all people" (v. 24). In other words, he did not believe in their faith. The rest of John's Gospel vindicates Jesus in his judgment of people who wanted him on their terms (see John 6).

In Mark 4, Christ explains the parable of the sower to his disciples. We learn that some "endure for a while" (v. 17) but fall away when suffering comes. John Calvin addresses the thorny theological problem of people falling away. He notes that Scripture explicitly testifies that elect children of God, those drawn by the Father (John 6:44) and led by the Holy Spirit (Rom. 8:14), can never fall away. Yet Calvin adds,

> To all this I answer, That God indeed favours none but the elect alone with the Spirit of regeneration, and that by this they are distinguished from the reprobate; for they are renewed after his image and receive the earnest of the Spirit in hope of the future inheritance, and by the same Spirit the Gospel is sealed in their hearts. But I cannot admit that all this is any reason why he should not grant the reprobate also some taste of his grace, why he should not irradiate their minds with some sparks of his light, why he should not give them some perception of his goodness, and in some sort engrave his word on their hearts. Otherwise, where would be the temporal faith mentioned by Mark 4:17? There is therefore some knowledge even in the reprobate, which afterwards vanishes away, either because it did not strike roots sufficiently deep, or because it withers, being choked up.[1]

In a similar vein, others have distinguished between a temporary faith and a historical faith. Robert Rollock says,

> The reason of the name is this; it is called *Temporary*, because it endures but for a time, because it hath no root. It hath the same object with justifying faith, and which is properly so called, namely Jesus Christ with his benefits, offered in the word of the Gospel and in the Sacraments; wherein it differs from historical faith, which hath for the object thereof the universal truth. It hath the same subject with justifying faith; for it hath its meat both in the mind, and also in the will and heart.[2]

Reformed authors by and large do not depict a spurious or temporary faith as something overtly false or of a beastly nature. They typically emphasize the powerful influence of the Spirit by and with the gospel on even the unregenerate. Such may be members in good standing in the church and appear to be true believers to themselves and others. Yet while enjoying spiritual benefits and participating in the worship of God, they lack salvation in Christ, which is marked by a supernatural faith that perseveres to the end.

In Hebrews 6, a well-known passage on Christian apostasy, we encounter what at first glance looks like a beautiful description of a Christian believer. However, we find out that those described in Hebrews 6:4–6 were never true believers savingly united to Jesus Christ. These temporary believers have "tasted the heavenly gift," "shared in the Holy Spirit," and "tasted the goodness of the word of God and the powers of the age to come" (vv. 4–5). That these qualities exist in those who have "fallen away" (v. 6) could lead us to believe (as some do) that these people lose their salvation. Yet in the context of Hebrews and the entire New Testament teaching on salvation by grace alone, we must conclude that they possess the appearance and not the reality of faith. They made an outward profession of their faith and even enjoyed certain spiritual benefits in connection with the church of Christ. But they nonetheless fall away (v. 6).

Note well that this passage does not teach that Christians can lose their salvation. Neither does this passage represent a purely hypothetical situation, as if to suggest, "If this were to happen (i.e., the spiritually enlightened fall away), *though it cannot, due to God's gracious gift*, it would be impossible to restore such people." Such a hypothetical argument would empty this passage of any real threat, contrary to what God intends for professing believers tempted to turn away from him.

Instead, we need to see in this passage that people enter into the full fellowship of the covenant community based on what has been called a "credible profession of faith." Simply, they possess a believable testimony of being a Christian. The elders often examine those professing faith to verify that their faith has deep roots in Christ (i.e., that faith works through love, Gal. 5:6). But we cannot know the heart, only the outward appearance of things. We cannot know infallibly that God elected this individual. Such we are not required to know. Only God knows this with certainty. We, as elders, simply try to ascertain whether someone has a true, lively faith that clings to Christ Jesus for both justification and sanctification.

The church and its elders can be wrong when examining candidates for membership. Yet they do not want to unnecessarily exclude a true child of God. Hence, we judge charitably the profession of faith by those who appear to possess true faith. In the fellowship of the church, some who appear to possess genuine faith but do not really may never manifest their true nature until years and years later—or maybe never in this lifetime. In the process they enjoy certain true spiritual blessings yet without possessing a saving interest in Christ. If they happen to turn away from Christ, they truly lose something but not salvation. Such they never attained. Concerning apostates, R. Fowler White helpfully observes that they "suffer real losses, but the losses they suffer do not include blessings they never actually had, namely, saving graces that flow from the decree of election."[3]

Naturally, given the complexity of sin and human nature, many profess who are not true believers. Their profession may be convincing, eloquent, and ultimately powerful. But if their faith lacks a supernatural saving quality, then their faith will ultimately fail, often with apostasy taking place in this life (Heb. 10:35–39).

Question 15

What is Satan's goal in his assaults on God's children?

Satan assaults God's children with the goal of getting them to forsake God and faith in him, especially through the neglect of the Word and prayer.

When Christ faced the Devil and his temptations in the wilderness, he provided an example for us when we are tempted. In short, Satan wanted Christ to abandon his trust in God in exchange for the way of ease and glory. We, like Christ, must live by faith and self-denial while assaulted by temptations of self-gratification at the cost of doing the will of God.

When Satan tempted Christ, he argued, "If you are the Son of God, command this stone to become bread" (Luke 4:3). Christ immediately turned to God's Word: "It is written, 'Man shall not live by bread alone'" (Luke 4:4, citing Deut. 8:3). By quoting this passage, Christ in faith manifested his awareness that he would be sustained by God's omnipotent hand, not by his own natural resources. God would supply his needs, of which his Word was the greatest. Satan attempted to supplant this spiritual priority with something physical. Temptations very often bring us to the place where we want to supply our own needs (often at the expense of something more important) rather than trust God to do so.

People have sometimes questioned whether the offering at church should be considered part of corporate worship. To this I answer an emphatic yes—and not simply because I get paid from it. In giving to the work of the kingdom, we are living by faith by giving up our own resources, trusting that God cares for us.

In Christ's second temptation, Satan tempted him to skip God's path of suffering to glory for something more immediate (and destructive) proposed by Satan. The Devil's promise of immediate glory (Luke 4:5–7) prompted Christ's response of dependence on God (Luke 4:8). We too encounter great difficulty on the path to glory. Satan tempts us to bypass the path of suffering for the ease of this-worldly temporal "glory." Serving the Lord—the first commandment—means traveling a path that looks like madness from the eyes of faith. But such a path of faith remains the only one worth taking since it alone leads to God.

In the Old Testament, the Israelites consistently tried to "prove God" (cf. Exodus 17; Deut. 6:16; 9:22; 33:8). The Israelites persistently struggled with unbelief in their walk with God (Ps. 95:5–11; Heb. 3:7–4:13). They failed to believe that he would bring them to the Promised Land (Ex. 17:7). The Devil tempted Christ to cast himself down in the expectation that God would send angels to protect him (Luke 4:9–11). Unlike the Israelites, Christ refused to put God to the test (Luke 4:12). When we depart from the life of faith, especially in the context of temptation, we put God to the test. We want him to protect us while we willfully enter into sin. By playing such games with God, we place ourselves in danger, for he never promises refuge in the context of our rebellion.

When we pray for God to keep us from temptation, we live by

faith while recognizing that Satan remains no match for God when it comes to power and protection. Faith tells us, "You cannot resist the powerful onslaughts of Satan, but in God you can. Go to him, crying out for help in your time of need" (cf. Heb. 2:18).

God will come to our aid in temptation if we go to him on a daily basis for deliverance from temptation (Matt. 6:13). We can endure every temptation because he can always provide a way of escape (1 Cor. 10:13). Peter claims that believers "by God's power are being guarded through faith for a salvation ready to be revealed in the last time" (1 Pet. 1:5). God keeps us in Christ, while we look to him (1 Pet. 1:6–9).

Christ challenges us, in the midst of his own Gethsemane temptations, "Watch and pray that you may not enter into temptation. The spirit indeed is willing, but the flesh is weak" (Matt. 26:41). He himself faced a greater and more powerful temptation in the garden than we will ever experience in our lives. The whole salvation of the human race depended on whether Christ would, by faith, accept the Father's will for him to joyfully suffer shame on the cross under the curse of almighty God. He stood firm in this and all temptations as a man of faith entrusting himself to his Father in his time of need.

As a result, the author of Hebrews can promise us, "For because he himself has suffered when tempted, he is able to help those who are being tempted" (Heb. 2:18). We cannot help ourselves in temptation. The idea that "God helps those who help themselves" is no truth at all, because we are utterly helpless in and of ourselves. Our help and strength come from Christ, who alone can give them. Faith looks to God for deliverance, not just in temptations but also before they arrive. Anyone wishing great strength in temptation must be much in prayer before temptation comes.

Question 16

How should we respond in the trials God sends us?

We should respond by faith in trials, which come
as gifts from a good, wise, and powerful God,
as he refines and perfects our faith.

God sends trials into our lives in order to test and nurture our faith. Indeed, patience is closely tied to the three theological virtues. As the sovereign Lord, he does all things well. The promise related by Paul in Romans 8:28, that "all things work together for good" to those who love God, comes in the context of the suffering life (Rom. 8:18–30).

Thomas Watson opens up Romans 8:28 and the topic of God's providential dealings in his *Divine Cordial*. He aims to treat this claim: "All the various dealings of God with his children, do by a special providence turn to their good." Such divinely tempered providences become a "cordial" for Christians, "like an invigorating medicinal drink concocted even with ingredients that may be poisonous by themselves." By themselves, trials are poisonous and hurtful to us, but in the hand of God they become medicinal and helpful. Such afflictions can be used, therefore, to teach us, make us more holy, conform us to Christ, draw us nearer to God, increase our happiness, silence the accusations of the wicked, and prepare us for glory.[1]

Peter also speaks of the "various trials" that come on his readers and reminds them that these trials prove the "tested genuineness" of their faith and "may be found to result in praise and glory and honor at the revelation of Jesus Christ" (1 Pet. 1:6–7). Likewise, James considers that the testing of faith produces steadfastness (James 1:3). Given that God brings such testing for our good, both James and Paul tell us to rejoice in the midst of it, with the latter claiming, "Not only that, but we rejoice in our sufferings, knowing that suffering produces endurance" (Rom. 5:3; cf. James 1:2).

In the Old Testament, faith is frequently put on trial (e.g., Genesis 22; Job), with afflictions likened to the refining process of gold (Job 23:10; Jer. 9:7; Zech. 13:9; Mal. 3:2). In this way, we see that faith is more precious than gold. No wonder, then, that the former, like the latter, must be tested and refined by the fire. Why does God test us and send painful trials into our lives? Because faith must be refined and nurtured as it grows up into maturity. Self-reliance must be burned away from our lives. This does not happen apart from trials and suffering.

The life of Job provides an excellent example of embracing trials while believing in a good, wise, and powerful God. Apart from faith, Job's life would have ended in despair. Instead, he could (with his struggles implied) claim,

> Behold, I go forward, but he is not there,
>   and backward, but I do not perceive him;
> on the left hand when he is working, I do not behold him;
>   he turns to the right hand, but I do not see him.

But he knows the way that I take;
> when he has tried me, I shall come out as gold.
> (Job 23:8–10)

In these remarkable words of faith in the throes of suffering, Job feels abandoned by God, as many of the psalmists do (e.g., Psalm 88). Yet he knows, even in the midst of the sheer pain, heartache, and terror of God's testing, that he will "come out" of the fire "as gold" (Job. 23:10). Eventually, Job gets to the place where he confesses,

> I know that you can do all things,
> and that no purpose of yours can be thwarted.
> "Who is this that hides counsel without knowledge?"
> Therefore I have uttered what I did not understand,
> things too wonderful for me, which I did not know.
> "Hear, and I will speak;
> I will question you, and you make it known to me."
> I had heard of you by the hearing of the ear,
> but now my eye sees you;
> therefore I despise myself,
> and repent in dust and ashes. (Job 42:2–6)

God aims to make us like his Son (Rom. 8:29; 2 Cor. 3:18). He not only turns sinners into saints; he also makes them Christlike in righteousness and holiness (Eph. 4:24), a task impossible for man but not for God. Sometimes the crushing blows of his trials are the result of his fatherly discipline (Heb. 12:5–11). Our Father uses the painful trial to yield the "peaceful fruit of righteousness" (Heb. 12:11). On this verse, Watson exclaims, "How much good comes to the saints by affliction! When they are pounded and broken, they send forth their sweetest smell. Affliction is a bitter root, but it bears sweet fruit."[2]

In their trials, Christians must consider and look to God. Joseph Caryl offers these words as if from Job's mouth:

Lord, though all this be come upon me, yet I will not depart from you, or deal falsely in your covenant. I know you are still the same Jehovah, true, holy, gracious, faithful, all sufficient; and therefore behold me prostrate before you, and resolving still to love you, still to fear you, still to trust you; you are my God still and my portion forever. Though I had nothing left in the world that I could call mine, yet you Lord alone are enough, yet you alone are all.[3]

In trials we must remember God's infinite goodness in all that he does for and to us. Likewise, we must never fail to see his infinite wisdom in that what he does transcends our understanding. Our trials may not make sense to us, but they always do in the mind of an all-wise God. Let us also always keep in mind his infinite power; he is ever capable of bringing good (cordial) out of bad (poison). He can and will work all things together for good for those whom he loves. But faith, and faith alone, embraces the God of Romans 8:28. When we feel as though everything conspires against us, faith keeps us believing that everything is working for us.

Consider Mary at the cross. Could she have envisaged anything worse than seeing her son crucified as a criminal and under the curse of God? Yet when she perhaps felt as though nothing worse could happen to her, the opposite unfolded before her, as a good, wise, powerful God worked what was best for her through his Son. Faith brings us to the place where we believe what William Cowper expresses so masterfully in his hymn "God Moves in a Mysterious Way" (1774):

Deep in unfathomable mines
Of never-failing skill
He treasures up his bright designs
And works his sovereign will.

Ye fearful saints, fresh courage take;
The clouds ye so much dread
Are big with mercy and shall break
In blessings on your head.

Judge not the Lord by feeble sense,
But trust him for his grace;
Behind a frowning providence
He hides a smiling face.

Question 17

Does true faith always persevere and end in victory?

Yes, faith, as a supernatural gift of God, perseveres to the end in victory, only because of Jesus Christ, who can never fail.

Abraham's faith gained the victory in the end. Hence, he takes his place as the father of those who believe (Rom. 4:11). His faith came under severe testing (Genesis 22) and ultimately proved victorious. All children of Abraham, by faith in Christ Jesus, will also emerge victorious in the end as their faith manifests itself as genuine. In the Westminster Confession, we are told that whether weak or strong in faith, all believers will triumph in faith: "This faith is different in degrees, weak or strong; may be often and many ways assailed, and weakened, but gets the victory" (14.3).

In the case of the greatest act of faith ever displayed, Christ went to the cross and cried out the words of dereliction but not without committing himself into the hands of God (Luke 23:46). He knew that upon death he would enter paradise. Faithful to the end, he accomplished a great victory over Satan (Gen. 3:15; Heb. 2:14). Even before the cross, his High Priestly Prayer—a copy of what takes place in heaven as he ever lives to intercede for the elect—shows the triumph of Christ as our faithful Savior.

Because we are united to Christ, we have confidence that our faith will triumph, as Christ possessed the same confidence. He bestows on us faith, because he himself possessed it. Christ is more confident in the victory of our faith than we are. To Peter he testified, "Simon, Simon, behold, Satan demanded to have you, that he might sift you like wheat, but I have prayed for you that your faith may not fail. And when you have turned again, strengthen your brothers" (Luke 22:31–32). Why does our faith not fail? Because Christ prays for us, just as he did for Peter. If he did not intercede for us, we would be defeated rather than victorious in our faith. We, then, are always to "take up the shield of faith, with which [we] can extinguish all the flaming darts of the evil one" (Eph. 6:16). Lifting up the shield remains our action, but the power to do so comes only from Christ.

Perhaps the most explicit words in the Scriptures regarding the victory of faith come from John: "For everyone who has been born of God overcomes the world. And this is the victory that has overcome the world—our faith. Who is it that overcomes the world except the one who believes that Jesus is the Son of God?" (1 John 5:4–5).

The new birth, also called *regeneration*, remains foundational for the victory. We do not overcome the world all at once. The life of faith leads us on to final conquest but not without bloody conflict and lost battles along the way. Being born of God secures the certainty of our triumph, but the possession of that triumph comes through a life lived by faith in the Son of God (Gal. 2:20).

In one respect, our faith acts out our victory as the instrument of it. Hence, the faithful win the prize based on many promises in Scripture. For example, James speaks of the man who remains faithful to the end receiving his reward: "Blessed is the man who remains steadfast under trial, for when he has stood the test he will receive the crown of life, which God has promised to those who love him" (James 1:12). To the church in Pergamum, Christ said, "Do not fear what you are about to suffer. Behold, the devil is about to throw some of you into prison, that you may be tested, and for ten days you will have tribulation. Be faithful unto death, and I will give you the crown of life" (Rev. 2:10). Suffering, trials, and faith remain part of the Christian life. But equally so is the promise of reward.

Jesus states clearly, "The one who endures to the end will be saved" (Matt. 24:13). We endure by the principle of faith. Such a "good gift" coming from the "Father of lights" above (James 1:17) can never fail. Supernatural faith leads to a supernatural end: glory. We walk by faith, not by sight, on a road of God's making. As brutal and perplexing as the road may be, we will make it to the finish line of glory. The trial and triumph of this grace comes in Christ Jesus, the pioneer and perfecter of our faith (Heb. 12:2).

Part 2

HOPE

Question 18

How is hope commonly understood?

Hope is typically seen as the optimistic
expectation that something will happen in
this life or the one to come, but this must
be distinguished from Christian hope.

Hope may be defined in worldly terms as a feeling of optimism or
a desire that something will happen, sometimes with a degree of
expectation. Everyone who lives long enough will experience many
different hopeful expectations. Often they hope for good health or
a good marriage or a good night out or a victory for their favorite
sports team. Many even have a type of religious hope whereby they
expect to enjoy heavenly felicity after death, but their grounds for
such hope are based on subjective personal feelings. Hence many
non-Christian funerals are filled with messages of hope: "He or she
is smiling down on us right now."

The natural man, who is outside Christ, may have a type of
hope, either limited to this world or presumptuous concerning
the world to come. This applies to non-Christians as well as to

hypocritical church attendees and members. All hope must rest on something, but the key question is whether God and his scriptural promises are that foundation on which we find refuge by the power of the Spirit.

Over the course of world history and even today, many religious people have erred by embracing a defective view of themselves and God. Once people fashion themselves into their own image (e.g., saying they are not that bad) and do the same with God (e.g., ignoring his holiness), all sorts of presumption creeps in about their eternal destiny. Yet this anticipation is based on a lack of true knowledge. Ignorance and hope are enemies. Knowledge of God in Christ emerges as the true friend of hope.

Many have hope of future bliss because, after all, God is love. "God," they say, "is interested in our well-being and will certainly care for us, because that's his job." Such hope might even lay claim to God's mercies, all the while forgetting that God reserves saving mercies for only repentant sinners. For those not thinking God's thoughts after him, love and mercy are fleeting concepts possessing little to no ground in divine revelation. But that does not matter to them, for this decidedly lopsided, wrong view of God assures them that they have procured what they want.

However, we cannot mess with the scriptural doctrine of God. Isolating one attribute from the others (as if they did not exist) has disastrous consequences. For example, consider Satan's tactics in the garden: "But the serpent said to the woman, 'You will not surely die'" (Gen. 3:4). Satan appealed to God's mercy and love in a way that exposes his lies about God. Many people can have hope of future joy, bliss, and heavenly existence but only because they presumptuously believe that God will do this or that since he is loving and merciful. Such thinking deceives them because they fail to recognize that God's mercy and love exist side by side with his justice and holiness, which shapes the very character of our hope.

Others place their hope not only in God's love but also in themselves. They are "spiritual mathematicians," believing that their good deeds outweigh their bad ones. They rarely consider the sins of the mind as bad deeds, focusing instead on external deeds, perhaps only the really heinous ones. Plus, they make generous estimations of themselves as righteous when in fact quite the opposite is true. Thus, their hope remains grounded in the fact that, coupled with God's love, they have done enough to warrant acceptance into his heaven.

The default position of the natural man is to think this way. Even deeply religious people seek to establish their own righteousness before God without ever truly submitting to his (Rom. 10:3). "Hitler, Stalin, and Mussolini should all be worried, but I'm not as bad as they were," reasons this type of person. "God will deal with the really wicked people of this world in some way, but the vast majority of us are good people trying to do our best in a difficult world." That is their hope. They believe that God is good but that people are too—and that is a match made in heaven. Consider one of the most solemn warnings in the Bible, from the lips of Christ himself, regarding the misplaced confidence of people who "do things":

> Not everyone who says to me, "Lord, Lord," will enter the kingdom of heaven, but the one who does the will of my Father who is in heaven. On that day many will say to me, "Lord, Lord, did we not prophesy in your name, and cast out demons in your name, and do many mighty works in your name?" And then will I declare to them, "I never knew you; depart from me, you workers of lawlessness." (Matt. 7:21–23)

Another class of people with false hope is occupied by those who have had some misfortune in the world. They may have suffered more than the average person. Or at least they think they have suffered more, perhaps because they are self-focused by nature and assume (often wrongly) that their troubles are worse than someone else's. However, as John Angell James provocatively and perceptively notes: "A life as long as that of Methuselah, spent in all the destitution and disease of Job upon his dunghill, would be no atonement for sin, and afford no ground to depend upon for salvation."[1]

Moving closer to the realm of the visible church, many of whose members are much like the people described above, we encounter those who put their hope in their denomination or membership. "I was born a Baptist, and I'll die a Baptist," we might hear them tout. But what does Jeremiah say? "Do not trust in these deceptive words: 'This is the temple of the LORD, the temple of the LORD, the temple of the LORD'" (Jer. 7:4). The temple would not keep the Israelites safe, and neither will being a Baptist, Anglican, or Presbyterian keep someone safe whose hope rises no higher than church membership and its privileges.

Others place confidence in the fact that they have been baptized. Looking to our baptism is a wonderful thing if, by faith, we embrace the promises expressed in it. Christians should constantly remember their baptism, as if it happened to them each day. For, in a manner of speaking, we are each day "baptized" insofar as the promises of our sins being washed away are daily realities. Looking to our baptism by faith is the same thing as looking to Christ.

Yet we are to improve on our baptism. The Westminster Larger Catechism asks, "How is our baptism to be improved by us?" (q. 167). The presumptuous person does not consider how he may improve on his baptism. He is concerned with the past event of the baptism (i.e., it happened) rather than the spiritual reality of the baptism (i.e., what it means for him). The true Christian should be considering not only the benefits offered to us in baptism but also what it means for us: we are sinners in need of a Savior. To the degree that we constantly embrace the promises of baptism, we can rightly place our hope in the waters of baptism.

Others place their hope in orthodoxy. They may be well versed in matters of doctrine and possess keen theological minds, having read many volumes by individuals such as Calvin, Owen, Edwards, Spurgeon, and Lloyd-Jones. One wonders how reading these men could leave someone in a state whereby they depend on sound doctrine and not on Christ himself, but I have seen it with my own eyes. Their knowledge becomes the object of faith and not Christ. Please do not misunderstand me, as I do not mean to say that doctrine is unimportant. However, some can make trust in their convictions rather than in Christ their basis for hope. Amazingly, they may place such a value on right doctrine that they may have faith in justification by faith alone and not in the Christ alone who justifies. Instead of having vital communion with the three persons of the blessed Trinity, they have communion with themselves, their doctrine, and the theologians they read.

How tragic when such a person comes so close and yet remains so far. In Matthew 7, Christ speaks to those who did many things in his name. But what is Christ's principal concern? He never knew them (Matt. 7:23). They knew theology, but they did not know the living God and his Son (John 17:3).

Finally, some put their hope in the fact that God's blessings in this life confirm the same in the life to come. To the church in Laodicea, Christ says, "For you say, I am rich, I have prospered, and I need nothing, not realizing that you are wretched, pitiable, poor, blind, and naked" (Rev. 3:17). The Laodiceans may have believed that their economic prosperity was a sure sign of their religious faithfulness and of God's blessing (cf. Hos. 12:7–13). We may understand events in our lives as blessings when in fact God views them as curses. Our hope cannot rest in circumstances, for God sometimes puts those he loves through poverty and suffering.

Question 19

What is Christian hope?

Christian hope is a Spirit-given virtue
enabling us to joyfully expect things
promised by God through Jesus Christ.

Christian hope is, regrettably, not a major part of our lives in contemporary Western society. Many of us live very comfortable lives. Many of us have never experienced hunger or homelessness. Perhaps in the future, should intense suffering come to the Western church, hope will find its rightful place in the Christian life as the necessary companion to faith.

Hope looks to God. Why? Because he is the "God of hope" (Rom. 15:13), the very "hope of Israel" (Jer. 14:8). Peter explicitly says, in light of the resurrection of Christ, that our "faith and hope are in God" (1 Pet. 1:21). The degree to which we find God desirable will be the same to which hope plays a role in our lives.

At just this point we encounter a typical problem among Christians, namely, the failure to go far enough in our desires for him. He has promised many blessings to his children, many of which are still unrealized. But we cannot simply hope in the blessings. We must hope in the God of the blessings.

Who is this God of hope? A small god begets small hope. A great God begets great hope. In fact, the psalmist describes the blessed person as the one "whose help is the God of Jacob, whose hope is in the LORD his God" (Ps. 146:5). The psalmist goes straight to him. But who is this God? He is the one "who made heaven and earth, the sea, and all that is in them, who keeps faith forever; who executes justice for the oppressed, who gives food to the hungry. The LORD sets the prisoners free" (Ps. 146:6–7). All that we can hope for from him depends on who he is and what he is able to do.

Thomas Aquinas makes this point beautifully:

> Wherefore the good which we ought to hope for from God properly and chiefly is the infinite good, which is proportionate to the power of our divine helper, since it belongs to an infinite power to lead anyone to an infinite good. Such a good is eternal life, which consists in the enjoyment of God Himself. For we should hope from Him for nothing less than Himself, since His goodness, whereby He imparts good things to His creature, is no less than His essence. Therefore the proper and principal object of hope is eternal happiness.[1]

Aquinas raises our joy because he raises our God. A great God, infinite in power, remains the source of great hope. And our hope is enriched further because we believe in a great God who reveals himself in the person of his Son, Jesus Christ.

God has given two principal gifts to his people: his Son and his Spirit. After giving them, in one sense he had nothing left to give. How can we possibly conclude this? Because all things come from God through the Son and the Spirit. In giving the Son and the Spirit to us, God most gloriously displays his love, goodness, mercy, grace, wisdom, power, patience, and so forth.

Question 19

Therefore, Christian hope looks not only to God as its object but to God in Christ. Peter tells his readers, "Therefore, preparing your minds for action, and being sober-minded, set your hope fully on the grace that will be brought to you at the revelation of Jesus Christ" (1 Pet. 1:13). Here, Peter has especially in mind something future. William Ames attests that the "conditions which normally characterize an object of hope—that it be good, that it lie in the future, that it be difficult, probable—are all found in the promises of God."[2] God promises future grace that will be revealed in Christ Jesus when he returns. If Jesus is the greatest gift given to us by the Father, then our grounds for hope must be both in God and in Christ.

Like Peter, Paul picks up on this Christological accent when describing how the Gentiles are included in the people of God as a result of his promises: "To them [i.e., the saints] God chose to make known how great among the Gentiles are the riches of the glory of this mystery, which is Christ in you, the hope of glory" (Col. 1:27). Our future hope of glory is based not only on the prospect of Christ's return but also on the reality that he is in us. Elsewhere, in connection with this truth, Paul wishes the following: "May the God of hope fill you with all joy and peace in believing, so that by the power of the Holy Spirit you may abound in hope" (Rom. 15:13).

Paul adds a further crucial element to our understanding of Christian hope. We "abound in hope" through the power of the Holy Spirit. Christian hope is therefore Trinitarian. We hope in the promises of God in Christ by the power of the Holy Spirit. Because of the objects of our hope (i.e., God and Christ) and the power in which we hope (i.e., the Holy Spirit), our hope bursts with joyful expectation. We are speaking not about probable hope or about mere conjecture concerning things future but about great certainty.

In Philippians, Paul highlights his hope in the midst of suffering:

> For I know that through your prayers and the help of the Spirit
> of Jesus Christ this will turn out for my deliverance, as it is my
> eager *expectation* and hope that I will not be at all ashamed, but
> that with full courage now as always Christ will be honored in
> my body, whether by life or by death. (Phil. 1:19–20)

Paul's joyful confidence or "eager expectation" exists even in
suffering. Even in the uncertainty of his future circumstances, which
may be life or death, he can rejoice because of the certainty of his
hope. His joy is contingent not on living but on honoring Christ,
whether by life or by death.

Job expresses a similar sentiment in his own suffering: "Though
he slay me, I will hope in him; yet I will argue my ways to his face.
This will be my salvation, that the godless shall not come before
him" (Job 13:15–16). Job gleans hope from his expectation of being
delivered (saved) by God. Whether Job in the Old Testament or
Paul in the New Testament, saints possess a confident, not an uncertain, hope, a holy expectation for a future in God's hands based
on his promises. God vindicates us as his people—something we
cannot do for ourselves.

But our expectation in God must be joyful, which alone quali-
fies as a scriptural hope. The fruit of the Spirit includes peace and
joy (Gal. 5:22), which cause us to abound in hope. Given the nature
of the promises made to us, our hope in them, as it flows from faith,
necessarily issues forth in joy. The Christian's true aim in this life is
to glorify God and enjoy him forever, which finds its foundation in
the hope of God and all that he promises.

In sum, hope consists in desiring God and his promises to us
in Christ. We have a confident expectation of receiving what is
promised because of where our hope lies: in God. When these elements are present, joy necessarily enters into our understanding of
Christian hope, for we are excited by what awaits us (1 Pet. 1:3–6).

Question 20

What gives rise to Christian hope?

Faith in God through Christ by the
Spirit gives rise to Christian hope.

Faith and hope have an intimate relationship with each other (Rom. 4:18–21; 5:2; 15:13; Gal. 5:5; Eph. 1:18–19; Col. 1:23; 1 Tim. 4:10; Heb. 11:1; 1 Pet. 1:21), with the former being the foundation of the latter. One cannot adequately hope in the God of hope without faith. We must believe in order to hope in what we believe.

Faith apprehends God's promises, while hope expects what he promises. Faith and hope both feed on his promises and help believers in times of trouble. These two graces are so similar that we often cannot distinguish them. But when they are properly grasped, there can be no doubt that hope is the daughter of faith.

The difference between the two is not always easy to discern. Simply put, faith believes, but hope waits patiently. Yet there is an aspect whereby faith requires patience. God is the object of hope, as it specifically focuses on his goodness to us in Christ. Faith not only looks to God but also trembles at his threatenings when appropriate. Hope remains free of such fear. Faith and love can relate to a present or future object, but hope looks to the future alone.

Hope relates to faith in terms of our expectations. Hope relates to love in terms of our desire. Love requires desire, so the more we desire the good, the more we will love it. Equally, hope requires desire. The more we desire what is promised, the more we hope for it.

Again, we must believe if we are to hope. Having been justified by faith, "we rejoice in hope of the glory of God" (Rom. 5:1–2). Again, hope connects to joy and springs from faith. Believing that Christ died for our sins and freed us from condemnation (Rom. 8:1), we possess hope for the future. We expect to be saved, because we believe we have been. The *already* of faith gives birth to the *not yet* of hope. Faith believes all that God has promised, but hope expects it.

Herman Ridderbos rightly claims,

> Hope is indissolubly bound up with faith . . . by virtue of faith's focus on Christ. . . . In all sorts of ways the apostle speaks of hope, together with faith and with knowledge (e.g., Col. 1:4ff.; Tit. 1:1ff.; Rom. 15:13), and in particular with faith and love, as giving expression to the whole Christian life (1 Cor. 13:13; 1 Tim. 1:3; Col. 1:4, *et al.*). Thus hope rests on faith (Gal. 5:5).[1]

We find an example of the interrelationship of faith and hope in the life of Abraham:

> In hope he believed against hope, that he should become the father of many nations, as he had been told, "So shall your offspring be." He did not weaken in faith when he considered his own body, which was as good as dead (since he was about a hundred years old), or when he considered the barrenness of Sarah's womb. No unbelief made him waver concerning the promise of God, but he grew strong in his faith as he gave glory

to God, fully convinced that God was able to do what he had
promised. (Rom. 4:18–21)

Paul tells us that Abraham believed against all hope in the sense
that he believed against what people in this world would ordinarily
think is impossible. There would be little or no hope for him from
the perspective of the person who lives "under the sun." But Abraham was God's friend. And so he had divine hope to bury human
hope. His hope in this instance was inextricably intertwined with
his faith in God and what he was able to do.

We may rightly say that Abraham was prepared to offer up his
son Isaac because of his great faith in God. But it was also because
he hoped (i.e., confidently expected) that "God was able even to
raise [Isaac] from the dead" (Heb. 11:19). Hence, "faith is the assurance of things hoped for" (Heb. 11:1). Future (good) events—
including the receiving of a son back from the dead—are made
certain by faith, which necessarily leads to hope. Or as J. Gresham
Machen observes, future events "become through faith so certain
that it is as though they had already taken place; the things that
are promised to us become, by our faith in the promise, so certain
that it is as though we had the very substance of them in our hands
here and now."[2]

Faith predicts the future, and if such is positive, we have hope
toward it. A negative future leads to despair, but because saving
faith embraces the promises of God, hope follows a bright future
for the Christian. Faith gives birth to hope, but other factors cultivate hope and strengthen it. Character produces stronger, more
God-centered hope (Rom. 5:4–5). Love toward God and neighbor
is also a friendly aid to our hope. And mortification of sin helps us
to grow in hope too. Yet hope emerges from a lively faith, which
necessarily fosters hope in the God who alone can give it.

Question 21

Is hope necessary for the Christian?

Yes, because we are born into a living hope through regeneration, this grace necessarily manifests itself in this life in expectation of good things from God.

Faith necessarily gives rise to hope in the human soul. Faith itself emerges from regeneration. Theologians debate whether faith precedes regeneration or regeneration precedes faith. The evidence of God's Word makes it clear that faith can never give birth to regeneration. Furthermore, the supernatural nature of faith makes it the consequence and not the cause of regeneration by the Spirit. Humans, in and of themselves, cannot exhibit supernatural faith. In the end, what would be the point of regeneration if we already possessed a supernatural gift from God through the Spirit?

At the beginning of his letter to "elect exiles of the Dispersion in Pontus, Galatia, Cappadocia, Asia, and Bithynia" (1 Pet. 1:1), Peter praises God because

> according to his great mercy, he has caused us to be born again to a living hope through the resurrection of Jesus Christ from

the dead, to an inheritance that is imperishable, undefiled, and unfading, kept in heaven for you, who by God's power are being guarded through faith for a salvation ready to be revealed in the last time. (1 Pet. 1:3–5)

Notice that Peter makes an inseparable connection between hope and the mercy of God. God has mercy on spiritually dead sinners because he realizes that their hope remains worthless apart from one produced by the regenerating power of the Spirit.

A true and living hope comes only to those made truly alive by the Spirit. God does this by a new birth, which may be called *regeneration*. He infuses into us supernatural habits, graces, and virtues. When this happens, God radically changes our world. We become creatures of hope. Geerhardus Vos makes an important point in connection with the hope into which we have been born:

The peculiar way in which the apostle expresses this fact ought to be carefully noted. He might have said, "God gave us a new hope," or, "God brought us into a new hope." But what he says is, "God begat us again unto a living hope." Undoubtedly this representation is chosen in order to emphasize the comprehensiveness and persuasiveness of the hope which the Christian obtains. It means a change as great as the crisis of birth; a transition from not being to living, when the hope of the gospel breaks upon our vision. The change is not partial. It does not affect our life in merely one or the other of its aspects. It revolutionizes our whole life at every point. What this means is a total regeneration of our consciousness, a regeneration of our way of thinking, a reversal of our outlook upon things in their entirety.[1]

As Christians who have been born unto a living hope, we experience a radical change in our worldview to the point that we both hope in good things to come and, more importantly, are governed by that hope. Theoretically, if God gives us spiritual life and knowledge of his being without also providing hope, we would be the most miserable of all creatures.

As soon as we come to savingly know God, we are filled with hope. For a Christian, to lack hope is to lack grace—an utter impossibility. Faith gives birth to hope. To take away hope is to eradicate faith.

Question 22

To whom is Christian hope given?

God gives this grace of hope both individually to the
Christian and corporately in the life of the church.

Christian hope finds its expression both individually and corporately. In a generally good treatise on faith, hope, and love, Peter Lombard makes two principal mistakes. First, he denies to Christ faith and hope, assuming that Christ possessed the beatific vision and so could not possess faith and hope.[1] Second, he claims that hope pertains only to the individual, whereas faith concerns both individual and corporate affairs.[2] Instead, Scripture portrays Christ as a man of faith, hope, and love. But also, as we shall see, hope (and not just faith) pertains to Christians both individually and corporately.

The theological virtues of faith, hope, and love cannot be properly cultivated by the individual alone. We require the household of faith to spur us on in our Christian walk. The Holy Spirit creates faith in individuals and then gathers them into the church, into which he pours forth the love of God. And where faith in Christ and love for God exist, you will find hope.

The church, as it manifests a unified hope, bears witness to the faithfulness of God, expressed by sending his Son to save sinners. The hope of one spurs on the same in others. The apostle Paul connects hope with character: "Character produces hope." He adds, "Hope does not put us to shame, because God's love has been poured into our hearts through the Holy Spirit who has been given to us" (Rom. 5:4–5).

As this passage bears out, the Christian can glory in tribulations because these sufferings are part of the sanctifying process that begins and ends in hope. Our tribulations as the people of God are designed to foster hope in our souls. But perhaps lost in all the glorious language of Romans 5:4–5, especially the emphasis on God's love being poured into our hearts, is the language of "us"! This is the language for the church.

Paul explains elsewhere, "If one member suffers, all suffer together; if one member is honored, all rejoice together" (1 Cor. 12:26). No individual member in the church should suffer alone, in a community whose members uphold and depend on one another. In the church, we belong to one another and suffer together, all because of our communion with Christ. As a result, when one hopes, we all hope together. Individual hope in the promises of God elicits not only individual but also corporate consequences.

Paul thanks the Thessalonians in his introduction: "We give thanks to God always for all of you" (1 Thess. 1:2). All these Thessalonians are then described as those who possess a "work of faith and labor of love and steadfastness of hope" in Christ (1 Thess. 1:3). What is true of one believer is assumed to be true of all. At the beginning of his letter to the Colossians, Paul also speaks of the three virtues:

> We always thank God, the Father of our Lord Jesus Christ, when we pray for you, since we heard of your faith in Christ

Jesus and of the love that you have for all the saints, because
of the hope laid up for you in heaven. Of this you have heard
before in the word of the truth, the gospel. (Col. 1:3–5)

Clearly, because of our hope, we love the saints. Christian hope has
corporate consequences.

Because we love those who are our brothers and sisters in the
Lord, we have a hope not only for ourselves but also for them. We
hope that they will also enter into the joy of the Lord. We hope
that they will, by faith, also wait patiently for their reward. Our
hope is in God, but that does not mean we cannot hope for others
to believe the God of hope. My confident expectation of my own
salvation in Christ is incomplete if my expectation remains solely
focused on myself. Indeed, he came to save individuals but not
simply such. He came to save them as part of a greater, comprehensive entity. He came to fetch his bride. We confidently expect that
Christ will usher in a new creation of loving people who believe
in his name. These people are those for whom I have great hope
in this life.

When we gather together to eat and drink the body and blood
of the risen Lord, who imparts his grace to us through his Spirit, we
bear testimony to our communal hope. No one should eat or drink
alone because no one should carry the burden of hoping alone. The
Lord's Supper is a corporate testimony of our faith, hope, and love:
faith to believe what is promised; hope to look forward to what is
promised; and love to God and Christ for what they have given to
us, the church. Since eating and drinking together strengthen the
church, we are privileged to have our hope increased when we dine
at the table of the Lord.

Question 23

How does hope relate to death?

Hope prompts us to cling to the promise that
when we die, we will be with Christ in paradise.

Hope looks to many promises. As Thomas Adams affirms,

> [Hope] tells the soul such sweet stories of the succeeding joys;
> what comforts there be in Heaven; what peace, what joy, what
> triumphs, marriage-songs, and hallelujahs there are in that
> country whither she is travelling, that she goes merrily away
> with her present burden.[1]

Yet these promises are not all received at once. Our right and title
to the promises of God are ours as soon as we believe, but our possession of the realities promised occurs in stages. Hence the doctrine
of hope: "For who hopes for what he sees?" (Rom. 8:24).

When we speak of heaven, we need to distinguish between the
intermediate state and life in the new heavens and new earth. We
generally refer to the intermediate state as a "disembodied" one.
John Angell James wisely comments, "The first object of Christian

hope . . . is an entrance into Heaven immediately after death."
He adds,

> I am aware that this is neither the sole nor the highest object
> of Christian hope and expectation; and that of course, the fe-
> licity of the Christian in his disembodied state, is not complete;
> and also that less is said about his entrance into glory at his
> death, than about the day of Christ's second coming. . . . Yet
> something is said about it, and therefore something should be
> thought about it.[2]

Indeed, something should be said about hope in relation to what
happens at death. The Westminster Larger Catechism asks, "What
is the communion in glory with Christ, which the members of the
invisible church enjoy immediately after death?" (q. 86). Answer:

> The communion in glory with Christ, which the members of
> the invisible church enjoy immediately after death, is in that
> their souls are then made perfect in holiness (Heb. 12:23), and
> received into the highest heavens (2 Cor. 5:1, 6, 8; Phil. 1:23;
> Acts 3:21; Eph. 4:10), where they behold the face of God in
> light and glory (1 John 3:2; 1 Cor. 13:12), waiting for the full
> redemption of their bodies (Rom. 8:23; Ps. 16:9), which even
> in death continue united to Christ (1 Thess. 4:14), and rest in
> their graves as in their beds (Isa. 57:2), till at the last day they
> be again united to their souls (Job 19:26–27).

Most of the time, the New Testament focuses on the eternal life
that believers enjoy after the intermediate state—life in the new
heavens and new earth. But there is, nonetheless, eternal "life after
death." Our hope has many promises on which to cast itself. As
the catechism makes clear, several promises are realized as soon as
we die: we are free from sin, we are in the highest heavens, and we

see God in Christ. The only promise left to be fulfilled is the resurrection of our bodies.

The conversation of Jesus with the thief on the cross shows us the glorious expectation of what we will experience at death. This man, who displayed great theological insight, received from Christ even richer doctrine: a theology of hope. As the criminal beside him railed at Christ, commanding him to save them all, the thief who was eventually saved rebuked the other criminal: "Do you not fear God, since you are under the same sentence of condemnation?" (Luke 23:40). He showed keen perception regarding the fear of God, but his theology got better. He admitted that the sentence they were receiving was a just sentence. In other words, he knew he was a sinner: "And we indeed justly, for we are receiving the due reward of our deeds; but this man has done nothing wrong" (Luke 23:41). He then displayed daring boldness, as a sinful man with God's judgment hanging over his head, to ask Jesus to remember him when he came into his kingdom (Luke 23:42).

Quite frankly, this is one of the greatest acts of faith displayed anywhere in God's Word. While so many of Christ's disciples had abandoned him because they doubted his identity as the Messiah sent to redeem Israel, this criminal affirmed an eternal kingdom that belongs to Christ. Think about that. He was putting his faith not in the resurrected Lord of glory but in a man under God's curse (Gal. 3:13). How did the dying Christ respond to all of this? He offered matchless hope: "Truly, I say to you, today you will be with me in paradise" (Luke 23:43).

We do not know how soon the thief died after this exchange, which remains a trivial question compared to the fact that Christ immediately imparted hope to a hopeless sinner. This is the beauty of the gospel. It takes the most hopeless situation (e.g., a crucified criminal) and offers the very opposite: hope! It matters little how much longer he lived. It matters most that he enjoyed unshakable hope in eternal life in the brief time he remained alive.

The thief had hope that death for him meant eternal life. Even better, he would enjoy life with Christ in paradise. When so many in the world are content to affirm life after death, even speaking generically of "heaven," how many focus on Christ at the center of heaven? How many, like the dying thief, believe that heaven is Christ's heaven and so want to be with him?

Without question, the dying thief displays one of the greatest acts of faith in the history of humanity. Christ rewards such faith with hope: a confident expectation of something good—eternal life—that finds its value in Christ alone.

All of God's people are expected to live in light of this promise, in hope that one day they will be with Christ in paradise. They will not enter into a state of unconsciousness or "soul sleep," as some have argued. They will immediately be ushered into the presence of Christ, who has been praying to his Father that his people would be with him and see his glory (John 17:24).

The process of dying can be very difficult, prolonged, hideous, and painful, even for Christians. Likewise, it remains heartbreaking for the loved ones of the one dying. But in death, the Christian, by the power of the Spirit and the promises of God's Word, possesses hope in the midst of even the greatest suffering. Life appears to rob the Christian of many things in this world, especially at death (e.g., dignity). Yet the Christian can never be stripped of the hope that at the moment he takes his last breath, he will be in paradise. In the end, all losses mean gain when a Christian dies, only to experience life eternal in the intermediate state and beyond. Consider John Owen's dying words:

> I am going to Him whom my soul loves, or rather who has loved me with an everlasting love, which is the sole ground of

all my consolation. . . . Live and pray and hope and wait patiently and do not despair; the promise stands invincible that he will never leave thee nor forsake thee.[3]

If we are able to speak when we come to die, our true theology will be revealed in the sense of what we really believe and what we really hope for. Many of us shall have an occasion to give a testimony in a moment (before death) to a life that took decades to live. Shall our living hope each day become a glorious testimony at our last day on this earth?

Question 24

What is the supreme object of Christian hope?

The supreme object of Christian hope is
Christ as seen face-to-face in his glory.

If someone you never met did great things for you, would you not want to meet that person? Job had faith and confidence that he would meet his Redeemer: "I know that my Redeemer lives, and at the last he will stand upon the earth" (Job 19:25). In light of the expectation of coming face-to-face with his Redeemer, Job exclaimed, "My heart faints within me!" (Job 19:27).

Since we live by faith and not by sight in this world (2 Cor. 5:7), we know Christ to a certain extent now. We know him by faith through the Spirit accompanied by and with the Word of God. United to Christ, we have communion with our risen Savior in heaven. That we will see Christ later does not preclude experiencing him now.

In the spirit of Augustine, communion involves the "enjoyment" and "possession" of the triune God. Regarding Christ, we delight in him now by the grace of Christ (2 Cor. 13:14), which is ascribed to him as subsisting in its fullness in him (John 1:14). The believer receives grace by receiving Christ. As John 1:16 testifies, "For from his fullness we have all received, grace upon grace."

Christians must understand that Christ possesses a peculiar and unique glory. The incarnation involves the union of the eternal Son of God with a human nature (body and soul). Upon his birth, Christ became the forever God-man, an incarnation that belongs to no other. The glory of his gospel remains intimately connected with identifying him as fully God and fully man. Only such a person could save sinners.

We think not only of who Christ is but also of what he came to do and what he presently does at the right hand of the Father. Such knowledge of his work on our behalf, which reached its pinnacle at Christ's death on the cross and resurrection from the grave, prompts in us not only joy unspeakable but also a love of the Savior. Such joy and adoration will only be satisfied fully when we see him face-to-face. Thus, there exists a sort of "frustration" in the Christian life while we wait by faith and in patience for the reward of our salvation, namely, beholding our Savior to whom we owe everything. God understands this and so promises to reward us with the very thing we desire most: the face-to-face vision of Christ. That is our hope. As Isaiah says,

> Your eyes will behold the king in his beauty;
>> they will see a land that stretches afar. (Isa. 33:17)

We behold Christ "in his beauty" by faith according to both his state of humiliation (Isaiah 53) and his state of exaltation (Psalm 110). In his state of humiliation, we see the beauty of his love for sinners, especially as he freely lays down his life for us. We see the beauty of his perfect obedience to the Father. We see the beauty of his Spirit-filled life in the context of so much hatred and animosity. All this we see by faith.

But the time will come when faith turns to sight. The time will come when hope fulfilled means beholding the King face-to-face in his heavenly beauty. Christ now possesses a type of beauty in his physical appearance that does justice not only to the beauty of his holiness but also to the fact that he is the visible image of the invisible God (Col. 1:15). Our hearts overflow with hope as we address our desires to Christ in heaven:

> You are the most handsome of the sons of men;
>> grace is poured upon your lips;
>> therefore God has blessed you forever. (Ps. 45:2)

The psalmist connects the "beauty" of the King with the "beauty" of his holiness:

> Your throne, O God, is forever and ever.
>> The scepter of your kingdom is a scepter of uprightness;
>> you have loved righteousness and hated wickedness.
> Therefore God, your God, has anointed you
>> with the oil of gladness beyond your companions.
>>> (Ps. 45:6–7)

Overall, this psalm manifests a lovely Trinitarian accent as God (the Father) anoints the King (Jesus) with the oil of gladness (the Holy Spirit). Thus, God's King experiences the peculiar privilege of being just that, the one and only eternal King in radiant beauty and matchless possession of the Holy Spirit.

In the New Testament, the apostle John explicitly connects the vision of Christ with hope: "Beloved, we are God's children now, and what we will be has not yet appeared; but we know that when he appears we shall be like him, because we shall see him as he is. And everyone who thus hopes in him purifies himself as he is pure" (1 John 3:2–3).

One day, we shall possess glorified bodies perfectly immune to corruption, decay, and death. Christ possesses such a glorified body already. His own hope, the immortality of his human nature, was fulfilled by God at the resurrection when he was raised in power (Rom. 1:4; 8:11). Our hope of immortality will be realized at the second coming of Christ when we shall see him.

The queen of Sheba heard much of Solomon's glory. But hearing of his glory was not enough for her. She had to see his glory:

> And when the queen of Sheba had seen all the wisdom of Solomon, the house that he had built, the food of his table, the seating of his officials, and the attendance of his servants, their clothing, his cupbearers, and his burnt offerings that he offered at the house of the LORD, there was no more breath in her. (1 Kings 10:4–5)

She finally saw his glory, and there remained "no more breath in her." In modern English, her experience of Solomon's glory "took her breath away." Her amazement was amazing.

Now consider what it shall be like for those who have longed for Christ's appearing (2 Tim. 4:8). If the queen of Sheba could say that that Solomon's glory surpassed the report she had been told (1 Kings 10:6–7), what shall we say when we are privileged to behold the Lord of glory? We currently know not a tenth or a hundredth or a thousandth—maybe not even a millionth—of what we will one day know of Christ's glory.

Hence, the supreme object of Christian hope is to see the risen Christ in his glory. For when we see him, we shall be like him. As those who are like him, we shall have all that our souls could possibly hope for.

Question 25

How does Christian hope relate to our future vision of Christ?

Our future vision of Christ necessitates the expectation for a resurrected body like his.

We all carry around bodies that fail to work as well as we would like.[1] We all experience infirmities that can at times be painful and debilitating. In reflecting on such maladies, we must remember that the fall brought sin and the misery that accompanies it to all people. Sin affects this world in a multitude of ways, not only spiritually but also physically. God never intended sickness, pain, disease, and death for humanity. These all have come because of sin. The longer we live, the more acutely we feel such effects on our bodies. Paul speaks to this problem in Romans:

> And not only the creation, but we ourselves, who have the firstfruits of the Spirit, groan inwardly as we wait eagerly for adoption as sons, the redemption of our bodies. For in this hope we were saved. Now hope that is seen is not hope. For who

hopes for what he sees? But if we hope for what we do not see, we wait for it with patience. (Rom. 8:23–25)

Believers, who possess the Spirit, cannot help but groan in this world of sin and misery. To be entirely comfortable in this world would raise serious questions about our faith, hope, and love. We groan for the fulfillment of our privileges as children of God, which includes the redemption of our bodies. We will one day be clothed with an immortal and incorruptible body. Since our citizenship is in heaven, we eagerly await the return of our Savior, Jesus Christ, "who will transform our lowly body to be like his glorious body, by the power that enables him even to subject all things to himself" (Phil. 3:21).

Based on what Paul says here, believers can expect that Christ's return will bring a dramatic transformation to the bodies of his people from "lowly" to "glorious." The "lowly" has in view these sin-stricken bodies that waste away (2 Cor. 4:16); the "glorious" has in view the likeness of our bodies to the exalted, glorified body of our Savior. There exists no higher or greater likeness than that of the visible image of the invisible God.

We currently possess bodies of sin (Rom. 6:6) or bodies of death (Rom. 7:24). In these passages the "body" represents the whole person—body and soul. Both stand in need of redemption. Christ assumed both body and soul because whatever he did not perfectly take upon himself cannot be redeemed in sinful humanity.

Our hope is not to be rescued from our current bodies but to experience the perfect healing (redemption) of them. This "healing" happens by way of transformation. Just as Christ's body was transformed in the grave by the power of the Spirit, so Christ will transform our bodies by that same power. God created our bodies and declared them good. Sin brought death and misery to all of us. Instead of simply destroying us and starting afresh, God chose to redeem our bodies and souls. We hope, then, not for redemption from creation but for the redemption of creation, of which we are the most glorious part (Rom. 8:20–25).

In terms of Christ's body, he emerges as the prototype. We learn about our "glorious bodies" as we consider Christ in his state of exaltation. Conformity to his body comes as the result of his exalted status as God's appointed King and as part of his reward. Paul calls Christ's resurrected body a "spiritual" body (1 Cor. 15:44), which does not refer to an immaterial, bodiless presence in heaven. Instead, it refers to a transformed and renewed body in heaven, one that is immortal and imperishable and incapable of ever dying again (1 Cor. 15:42, 52–55).

Not only Christ's body but also his affections are "spiritual." According to Thomas Goodwin, Christ's affections work not in his soul only but also in his body, "as their seat and instrument." However, the body is "so framed to the soul that both itself and all the operations of all the powers in it are immediately and entirely at the arbitrary imperium and dominion of the soul."[2] In other words, the infirmities in Christ's human nature on earth, experienced in terms of hunger and weakness, do not now affect his soul in heaven because his body is raised in power. The power of his body and soul are in perfect harmony because they are together "powerful," not weak or threatened by the curses of the world.

Following from this, Goodwin notes that the affections of pity and sympathy move Christ's "bowels and affect his bodily heart" in his states of both humiliation and exaltation. However, in heaven Christ's affections do not affect him in a negative manner as they did on earth in his humiliation and under the misery of sin. They "do not afflict and perturb him in the least," Goodwin argues, "nor become a burden and a load unto his Spirit, so as to make him sorrowful or heavy." This is so because Christ's human nature is "impassible" insofar as he cannot experience any hurt, now that he is in his glorified state (i.e., Jesus no longer weeps). Jesus is still compassionate and merciful, and thus his perfection does not destroy his affections "but only corrects and amends the imperfection of them."[3] Perfected passions are now in Christ (cf. Heb. 2:10; 5:7–10; 7:28).

Though Christ has shed affections that are incompatible with or unsuitable to his state in heaven, he nonetheless possesses other affections with a "greater capaciousness" and "vastness" that more than make up for his lack of former affections. In fact, Goodwin argues that just as Christ's knowledge was "enlarged" in heaven, "so his human affections of love and pity are enlarged in solidity, strength, and reality. . . . Christ's affections of love are as large as his knowledge or his power."[4]

How does this relate to us? Our glorified bodies will be free from the oppressive nature of sin. We love now, but we shall love a great deal more in heaven. Love brings joy, and joy brings love. In glory, we will have no capacity for sorrow, which does not mean that we will not cry with tears of joy upon seeing Christ. But we shall be freed from oppressive passions (i.e., tears of sadness, grief). We shall have not only incorruptible bodies that are going to live for eternity but also purified souls—both free from sin and positively righteous. Christ must never be considered simply as sinless—though he certainly is—but also as righteous. We shall be like him in body and soul.

How can this future promise not cause wondrous excitement in Christ's people at what awaits us? When we partake of the Lord's Supper in church, we should remember that his body was given in sacrifice for us so that our bodies might be healed in glory and for his glory. When we are sick, we must remember our future hope of a glorious body that will never be sick for all eternity. When we are weak, distressed, sad, and crying buckets of tears, we must put our hope in Christ's appearance:

Beloved, we are God's children now, and what we will be has not yet appeared; but we know that when he appears we shall be like him, because we shall see him as he is. And everyone who thus hopes in him purifies himself as he is pure. (1 John 3:2–3)

Question 26

In what destination do we
long to live forever?

We long to live forever in the new heavens and new
earth, communing with the Father, Son, and Holy
Spirit and with each other through the Spirit.

Many Christians are not as excited by the thought of heaven as
they should be. They know their hearts should be more affected
by the prospect, but they do not really fancy playing a harp in the
sky somewhere forever and ever in a white robe. With my limited
musical abilities, I remember a time when I sort of dreaded the
thought of being a musician in heaven forever, even if my musical
talent vastly improved.

My problem, and that of so many Christians today, was a
"Greek" (or Platonic) view of heaven, which is all spirit but no
body. However, coming to a better and more informed knowledge
of heaven can completely change the desires of Christians, to the
point that they really can say with the apostle Paul, "To live is
Christ, and to die is gain" (Phil. 1:21). With a view of heaven that

is more biblical, our hope to be with him in the new heavens and the new earth is one of holy intensity. For we know we will be spending eternity in a place that does justice to our whole humanity, not only our souls but also our bodies.

The picture of the new heavens and new earth in Revelation 21–22 should fill all Christians with hope and joy. Christ's enemies are put under his feet definitively and permanently. God reveals to John a picture of the eternal home of Christ and his bride. John likely gives a figurative rather than a literalistic description of the new earth. Nonetheless, the earth will be renewed (see Rom. 8:18–23).

In fact, God's original purposes for humanity are highlighted in the beginning chapters of Genesis. For all the beauty we read of in the garden of Eden, it would be deficient as a residence for the King of kings and Lord of lords. Christ deserves a cosmic "garden." We will return to the garden, so to speak, but we will return to Christ's garden. "Back to the future" is one way to look at God's purposes for humanity. Consider the language of Revelation 22, where in the new earth believers will commune with the Lamb of God face-to-face:

> Then the angel showed me the river of the water of life, bright as crystal, flowing from the throne of God and of the Lamb through the middle of the street of the city; also, on either side of the river, the tree of life with its twelve kinds of fruit, yielding its fruit each month. The leaves of the tree were for the healing of the nations. No longer will there be anything accursed, but the throne of God and of the Lamb will be in it, and his servants will worship him. They will see his face, and his name will be on their foreheads. And night will be no more. They will need no light of lamp or sun, for the Lord God will be their light, and they will reign forever and ever. (Rev. 22:1–5)

John clearly uses Ezekiel 47:1–9 here, but the imagery goes back even further to the garden of Eden. For example, in Genesis 2:10 we read, "A river flowed out of Eden to water the garden, and there it divided and became four rivers." The end will be like the beginning, except better and grander.

The New Jerusalem will be "the dwelling place of God" with his people (Rev. 21:3). In the original garden, God walked with Adam (Gen. 2:15; 3:8). Adam was God's prophet, priest, and king. The Lord directed Adam to fill the earth and subdue creation, but the man failed to execute his threefold role. So another "Adam" (i.e., Christ) was tasked with this responsibility, namely, to fill (Matt. 28:18–20) and subdue the earth (1 Cor. 8:6; 15:25–27).

By completing the work the Father gave him to do, Christ has brought his people back to Eden. Whatever delights Adam enjoyed in Eden will be magnified beyond our current comprehension because we will be in a far better situation than Adam. Whereas Adam was not guaranteed perpetual, eternal life in Eden, all those who belong to Christ can be assured of their perpetual, eternal life in the new earth. We also will "see his face" and thus commune with God through Christ, as well as commune with all those who shall be to us our eternal brothers and sisters in the Lord.

We who are in Christ are returning to this recreated earth for the simple reason that it belongs to Christ, who subdued it. But what we see now is only a small taste of what is to come. At that time, joy unspeakable will fill our hearts with the reality that we have finally found our eternal home on earth. Hence, Christian hope looks forward to the new earth where Christ will be our King and where we will, with him, be more than conquerors.

Question 27

Of what use is hope in times of suffering?

In suffering, hope comforts our souls and
allows us to live patiently while the church
waits for her entrance into glory.

Hope provides a foundation for Christian patience, which emerges as a fruit of the Spirit (Gal. 5:22). Furthermore, in our loving and joyful patience, we eagerly hope. Trials from the Lord heighten the grace of hope in our patient endurance. In turn, this patience is tied up with Christian character, and "character produces hope" (Rom. 5:4). Christian patience rests at the core of faith, hope, and love. Hope also acts as the "sweetest" friend of Christian patience, especially where suffering and trials are concerned.

Paul does a remarkable job of pastorally applying the grace of hope to suffering in the Christian life. Such sufferings are nothing compared to the glory to come (Rom. 8:18). If even the creation waits to be freed from its present bondage, how much more the children of God, who are aliens and strangers in this creation?

We believers, "who have the firstfruits of the Spirit, groan inwardly as we wait eagerly for adoption as sons. . . . For in this hope we were saved" (Rom. 8:23–24). This adoption of which Paul speaks will occur at the final consummation of all things, when God's people shall be publicly presented as the children of God. This does not deny that we are declared God's children as soon as we believe. And this by no means minimizes the groaning or sufferings of this present life. We hope for what we do not and cannot see (Rom. 8:25). But we patiently wait in the midst of our ongoing trials brought by God, who desires to conform us to the image of his Son.

John Owen argues that the "especial object of hope is eternal glory" (cf. Rom. 5:2; Col. 1:27). But the "peculiar use" of hope is to "support, comfort, and refresh the soul, in all trials, under all weariness and despondencies, with a firm expectation of a speedy entrance into that glory, with an earnest desire after it."[1] We can bear the trials God sends us not only because of the present grace he gives us (2 Cor. 12:9) but also because of the hope we have of future joy, blessedness, and glory.

The apostle Paul tells the Thessalonians that he remembers before God their "work of faith and labor of love and steadfastness of hope in our Lord Jesus Christ" (1 Thess. 1:3). Faith, hope, and love are all spoken of here. All three prepare us to take up our cross and live the life of the cross (e.g., self-denial, shame, suffering). How can we be prepared to live the cross-shaped life apart from faith, hope, and love? It is impossible.

The hope of many persecuted Christians becomes "very large" because of the situation in which they find themselves. Persecution promotes hope. That is one of the silver linings of living in a world where hatred of Christ goes beyond mere intellectual disagreements. Those whose lives are at risk because they bear the name Christian are those whose hope must be something that we in the West right now can only marvel at.

The apostle Paul knew what it was like to live a life of constant, intense persecution of his body and soul. But he was still able to write to the Corinthians,

> So we do not lose heart. Though our outer self is wasting away, our inner self is being renewed day by day. For this light momentary affliction is preparing for us an eternal weight of glory beyond all comparison, as we look not to the things that are seen but to the things that are unseen. For the things that are seen are transient, but the things that are unseen are eternal. (2 Cor. 4:16–18)

Paul does not explicitly use the word *hope* here, but his hope carries those words to the Corinthians as words to live and die by, not as mere pious platitudes. Similarly, those who suffer physically, perhaps through illness, cling to hope: hope that one day they will never have to worry about infirmities, tears, distress, or sadness. When we suffer, we hope. To the degree that we are free from trials on this earth, our hope tends to decrease, as we are tempted to become too comfortable with the temporal delights of this world. If God did not try us, we might be strangers to Christian hope and might not know how precious it is to those who suffer.

Thomas Adams speaks well about the glory of hope for the suffering saint: "Hope is the sweetest friend that ever kept a distressed soul company; it beguiles the tediousness of the way, all the miseries of our pilgrimage."[2] The sweetest friend indeed.

One of the most difficult spiritual graces to learn is patience. Patience is a fruit of the Spirit (Gal. 5:22), which means it is a gift given to God's people. But this gift is not an "easy" gift. Thankfully, alongside patience God gives the grace of hope to keep us patient. Patience would be practically impossible without hope. So for every "difficult" gift we receive, God gives us a suitable "helper."

What hope do we have regarding the salvation of our children?

We have great hope regarding the salvation
of our children, because a promise is made
to them, and they belong to the Lord.

In the beginning, God intended to fill the earth with creatures who loved and feared him. Adam and Eve received the responsibility of filling the earth with God's children. The temple of Eden would have spread to all ends of the earth. Adam, by sinning, failed to fulfill God's original intention. But that did not alter God's desire to fill the earth with his children. In Matthew 28, echoing the idea of the original "Great Commission" ("Be fruitful and multiply and fill the earth and subdue it," Gen. 1:28), Christ sends out his apostles to make disciples of all nations.

God's purposes do not fundamentally change, even if the means to accomplish his purposes do. God has always determined to have a people, and when sin jeopardized that, he fulfilled his determination through Christ. In the Old Testament, a principle of "to you and your children/seed" continues the basic pattern God etched into creation. For example, in God's promise to Abraham, which has worldwide implications, he says,

> And I will establish my covenant between me and you and your offspring after you throughout their generations for an everlasting covenant, to be God to you and to your offspring after you. And I will give to you and to your offspring after you the land of your sojournings, all the land of Canaan, for an everlasting possession, and I will be their God. (Gen. 17:7–8)

In other passages, God's Word affirms the "seed" promise (e.g., Ex. 6:1–8; Deut. 29:9–15; 2 Sam. 22:51; 23:5; Ps. 89:3–4). Thus, when he makes a covenant with his people, he always includes their "seed" (i.e., children). This is how God "works."

For God to work this way necessitates consistency with his original plan for humanity. Grace does not destroy nature. Rather, grace heals fallen nature. God restores his relationship with and intentions for fallen humanity through grace.

In light of this principle, we have more, not less, reason to believe that God's purposes toward our children in the new covenant are just the same as they would have been (hypothetically speaking) to Adam's children before the fall. Thus, when preaching his sermon at Pentecost to Jewish hearers, Peter reaffirms the *seed* principle as part of his gospel message: "For the promise is for you and for your children and for all who are far off, everyone whom the Lord our God calls to himself" (Acts 2:39).

Of course, the words "calls to himself" cannot be glossed over. However, the only reason Peter should have said to his Jewish hearers, "and to your children," is if they were still partakers of God's covenantal promises. There would have been no need to say, "and to your children," if God did not intend to make firm promises to them. Peter could have simply said, "For the promise is for you and for all who are far off, everyone whom the Lord our God calls to himself." But those in the Jewish community, who always understood their children to be heirs of the covenant promises made to Abraham, would have naturally understood Peter to be including their children in the new covenant. In fact, everything he says in Acts 2:39 remains consistent with God's scope of promises to Abraham in Genesis 17.

The children of believers are in a much more blessed position than the children of unbelievers. Our children ought to be raised from the womb praying, singing, worshiping, learning, and fellowshiping in the context of the church. God makes promises to them, but they are made in the context of the church, the covenant community, where they will be nourished with God's Word.

God can make promises to redeemed parents because their children receive various means of grace, such as the preaching of God's Word. He applies salvation to his people through means and not apart from them. The children of Muslims or Jews or atheists do not have the covenant promises because their context makes such promises unintelligible. The exact opposite holds true for our children. God's covenant promises make sense in light of his plan for saving sinners through the preaching of the Word.

His faithfulness to such promises showered on our children stirs our faithfulness to them, whom he has given to us. To be sure, there are and will be those children who depart from the faith. Such apostasy does not mean that they lose their salvation. But what they leave behind are true spiritual blessings from a faithful covenant God. Such losses have always been the case from the time of Adam's children onward. But that has not changed God's determination to save through families. Hence, his promises are the ground for our hope that our children will be manifested as our eternal brothers and sisters in the new creation.

Question 29

May we have hope regarding
the death of infants?

A Christian parent may have a confident hope
that his or her child dies in the Lord.

Many Christian parents face the reality of children dying in the womb or in infancy.[1] The harsh realities of sin can be very painful to those who lose loved ones, especially loved ones they never had the chance to get to know and enjoy. With such calamities in mind, can we offer hope and comfort to parents whose child dies in infancy?

Certain Reformed confessions since the Reformation have addressed this issue. Well-known preachers and teachers such as Charles Spurgeon and Benjamin Warfield have also offered their views. For example, in a sermon on 2 Kings 4:26, Spurgeon says, "As for modern Calvinists, I know of no exception, but we all hope and believe that all persons dying in infancy are elect."[2] Spurgeon may have been overstating his case here, but he seems to widen the scope considerably to also include persons dying in infancy who do not have Christian parents. We must be careful not to let sentimentality creep in at the expense of what the biblical data offers us.

If we hold to the doctrine of original sin, which includes Adam's imputed guilt, then we cannot speak of an "innocent child" in the eyes of God. Before him, who has "purer eyes than to see evil and cannot look at wrong" (Hab. 1:13), all infants are corrupt before God at conception (see Job 14:4; 15:14; Ps. 51:5; Rom. 5:12–21).

It's important to remember that being condemned to hell comes not simply because of people's actions but also because of who they are in the sight of God. They are sinners who do not have the blood of Christ to wash away their sins. For those who remain "in Adam," they will be unholy and profane before God. In this light, we cannot speak of an "age of accountability," because that misses the point of who we are by nature.

Some people "hope" that God will save all infants who die in infancy because he is a "God of love." But he is love only insofar as this attribute is consistent with all his other attributes (e.g., his holiness, his justice). So we must be very careful to avoid abstracting an attribute and making it into our own image in order to satisfy our theological proclivities. Remember, many have used the "God is love" mantra to defend universalism, annihilationism, and even homosexual unions. Many suppose a God of love would never do certain things, but such an assumption runs contrary to God's Word. For example, as horrifying as this sounds, the flood in Noah's time engulfed many young children who were drowned by the waters of judgment.

The Scriptures, in both the Old and New Testaments, plainly distinguish between the infants of believers and the infants of unbelievers. Christians are privileged to have children who are "holy" (clean, sanctified), while the children of unbelievers are not "holy" but "unclean" (1 Cor. 7:14). What the New Testament says about our children in comparison to the children of unbelievers, the Old Testament testifies concerning Israelite children in comparison to the unclean children (sometimes called "dogs," Matt. 15:26) of the surrounding unclean nations.

An Old Testament example that proves this point is found in Deuteronomy 20, where God commands the destruction of (unclean) children (Deut. 20:16–17; see also Joshua 6; 1 Samuel 15). We might think that the destruction of these pagan children seems harsh and unloving. But these children, including the infants, would likely have grown up to engage in the "abominable practices" of their parents (Deut. 20:18; cf. Ps. 137:8–9; Isa. 13:16). The seed of every known sin resides in the heart of an infant.

It seems as though some who speak to this issue do not adequately consider the biblical data. God's love does not contradict his justice or mean he will not judge sinners. Corporate solidarity, whether in community or family, is a major part of biblical teaching.

Having said all this, in an attempt to be faithful to the teaching of the Scriptures, we cannot say that the infants of unbelievers will definitely go to hell. Neither can we say that they have any guarantee of going to heaven. Approaching this question with caution and without overconfidence remains wisest.

We can and should speak more definitively to this issue when it comes to the children of believers. The Canons of Dort, which truly are the most ecumenical of all the Reformed confessions, address the topic of children dying in infancy:

> Since we are to judge of the will of God from his Word, which testifies that the children of believers are holy, not by nature, but in virtue of the covenant of grace, in which they, together with the parents, are comprehended, godly parents have no reason to doubt of the election and salvation of their children, whom it pleases God to call out of this life in their infancy. (first head of doctrine, art. 17)

The basis for having this hope comes not merely from the goodness of God but from his goodness as revealed in his covenantal promises toward his people. The children of believers are holy, and thus their identity is not, as far as we are to judge, "in Adam." They have been set apart, with a new identity (i.e., they are holy). The issue before us concerns our ability to extend charity while making sound judgment, not our ability to infallibly know the decree of God. His Word seems to give us some grounds to make these judgments, which, as a pastor, I am glad to offer to bereaved parents who have lost an infant.

In short, our identity (as justified children of the Father), not our works, remains the primary basis for where we end up in eternity. How does this relate to abortion? The great tragedy of abortion is that it robs a child of the privilege of hearing the gospel and being saved from this world of sin and misery. In the case of infants of unbelievers, this is especially tragic. Why? Once we grasp that God could, based on his righteous nature and on the guilt of infants in Adam (i.e., original sin), send these children to hell, we are faced with the true horror of abortion. Christians understand the eternal consequences involved in any human life. We have the greatest reasons to be against abortion.

Again, I am not saying that God sends the children of unbelieving parents to hell. But I am saying that the Scriptures do not give us quite the grounds that some (e.g., Spurgeon) think for guaranteeing the salvation of such children. This view might lead to a sort of "happy guilt" (*felix culpa*)—"abortion is bad, but at least they all go to heaven"—type of attitude. However, since we can't know, and as the stakes are so very high, we should aim to end abortion in order that we can aim to win these children to Christ.

The Westminster Confession of Faith says, "Elect infants, dying in infancy, are regenerated, and saved by Christ, through the Spirit" (10.3)—a view that could still *allow* for all infants, without exception, to receive salvation but without *demanding* that all infants will necessarily be saved. Certainly, the Westminster divines, based on the Directory for Public Worship, which calls the children of believers "Christians," would have likely been in agreement with the Canons of Dort on this issue.

Pastors have grounds for giving real comfort to Christians suffering the tragedy of losing a child, especially an infant. Perhaps David's words after losing the child he had with Uriah's wife, Bathsheba, are such grounds: "But now he is dead. Why should I fast? Can I bring him back again? I shall go to him, but he will not return to me" (2 Sam. 12:23). David's child was a covenant child. Some suggest that David simply meant that he would one day die and so go to be with the child "in the earth." But the words "I shall go to him" are words of hope, not despair.

This is the David who has resurrection hope (Ps. 16:10), and who says elsewhere, "But the steadfast love of the LORD is from everlasting to everlasting on those who fear him, and his righteousness to children's children" (Ps. 103:17). How David can have confidence in the midst of his sin teaches us how great the grace of God truly is. Joyce Baldwin says, "David comes to terms with his own mortality, and even in that finds hope, because he looks forward to being reunited with his child."[3]

There is a gospel typology in this tragic story: David is delivered but not without God punishing David's son. David had sinned, but his son's death is a type of "substitutionary death." The death of David's child led to David's "new life." David was, in a faint way, "resurrected," and life continued for him. Similarly, the Son of God receives the penalty for our tragic sins, and as a result, we are set free to newness of (resurrection) life. David's son is, amid the tragedy, a type of Christ, and thus we have further evidence that he went to be with the one of whom his (short) life spoke so richly.

In other words, there is soteriology (God's saving grace) all over this incident. David is, in the midst of tragedy, comforted with hope. Because of the limited biblical teaching on this subject, I cannot confidently offer that same comfort to an unbeliever. Yet that does not mean an unbeliever's child cannot be elect. It only means that I do not possess grounds for covenantal consolation.

Those who do not see a covenantal difference between the infants of believers and those of unbelievers must understand the ramifications for such a position. A concrete example is the difference between the children of Muslim parents and those of Christian parents. For this reason, some espouse a sort of universal salvation for infants who die. But returning to our example, are we really to conclude that both groups are on equal ground before God? In one respect, I find the *all infants* view appealing. However, this position lacks the explicit biblical teaching necessary to establish it.

Naturally, there are many other questions that arise when discussing this issue. Yet regardless of where we stand, there are important practical consequences for what we believe. We certainly can all say, "Shall not the Judge of all the earth do what is just?" (Gen. 18:25).

Question 30

What duty flows out of Christian hope?

Those who hope in God purify themselves.

There are many positive aspects to the life of hope: the expectation of eternal life (Titus 1:2; 3:7), salvation (1 Thess. 5:8), heaven (Col. 1:5), the resurrection (Acts 23:6), the gospel (Col. 1:23), God's calling (Eph. 1:18; 4:4), and our inheritance (Eph. 1:18). Yet notwithstanding all these "positive" promises in regard to Christian hope, there exists what we might call a "negative" side to Christian hope: "And everyone who thus hopes in him purifies himself as he is pure" (1 John 3:3).

The command to purify ourselves comes immediately after one of the greatest promises of Christian hope: "Beloved, we are God's children now, and what we will be has not yet appeared; but we know that when he appears we shall be like him, because we shall see him as he is" (1 John 3:2). To those who have the hope of being made like Christ in body and soul, they must also have the present desire to be *pure*. While in sanctification the accent is on what God does, here in 1 John 3:3, the accent is on what we do. Christians, if they embrace a hope of seeing Christ face-to-face, are to purify themselves.

Here we are dealing with the moral effect of Christian hope. The language of 1 John 3:3 makes clear that the pursuit of purity arises out of our possession of hope. Hope gives birth to sanctification, not vice versa.

Not only does John connect our future hope to present sanctification, but Peter and Paul do the same. Peter speaks of the future promise of the new heavens and new earth to his readers (2 Pet. 3:13) and then reasons, "Therefore, beloved, since you are waiting for these, be diligent to be found by [God] without spot or blemish, and at peace" (2 Pet. 3:14). In his exhortation, Peter focuses on our responsibility in sanctification. As Jonathan Edwards notes regarding sanctification,

> We are not merely passive nor yet does God do some, and we do the rest. But God does all, and we do all. God produces all, and we act all. . . . God is the only proper author and fountain; we only are the proper actors. We are, in different respects, wholly passive and wholly active.[1]

With almost identical language of purification, Paul writes to the Corinthians, "Since we have these promises, beloved, let us cleanse ourselves from every defilement of body and spirit, bringing holiness to completion in the fear of God" (2 Cor. 7:1). The promises Paul speaks of include our adoption as sons and daughters, wherein God makes his dwelling and walks among us (2 Cor. 6:16, 18). These promises are, of course, realized in this life but also await a type of consummation that we can all look forward to (see Rom. 8:23).

Christian hope has present realities, one of which includes our sanctification. In this matter, our faith clings ever so tightly to our hope, as we seek to be holy as God is holy.

Speaking of the nature of faith in justification, Herman Bavinck insists that faith manifests itself "only from its receptive side because in this connection everything depended on the acceptance of the righteousness offered and bestowed in Christ." Even so, "at the same time as it is justified, it was also a living, active, and forceful faith that renewed people and poured joy into their hearts."[2] Our faith, which in its very nature includes hope, is accompanied by ongoing repentance.

In connection with what we noted above relating to God's and our roles in sanctification, we can speak of both *passive* and *active* sanctification. The believer actively works out all things while God works in the passive believer to will and to do of his good pleasure (Phil. 2:12–13). As Bavinck notes, believers are passive when they are sanctified (John 17:19; 1 Cor. 6:11); indeed, "they died with Christ and were raised with him (Rom. 6:4ff.)." Christians are described as saints, "because by being called they stand in a special relationship with God."[3] That said, sanctification

> is not exhausted by what is done for and in believers. Granted, in the first place it is a work and gift of God, a process in which humans are passive just as they are in regeneration, of which it is the continuation. But based on the work of God in humans, it acquires, in the second place, an active meaning.[4]

This sanctification is "continued repentance," which denotes a dying to the old self or mortifying of the misdeeds of the flesh (Rom. 8:13). In the end, the Bible "insists on sanctification, both its passive and active aspects, and proclaims both the one and the other with equal emphasis."[5]

Those who hope are those who actively pursue holiness. In other words, we live for God's glory not simply because of what Christ has done for us but also because of what God in Christ will do for us one day. As Thomas Manton says,

> Why are God's children so hard at work for God, but out of love to him, and hope to enjoy him forever? Oh! Let us con-

tinually be serving God. Let us live always either for Heaven, as seeking it, or upon Heaven, as solacing ourselves with the hopes of it; do whatever we do in order to eternal life, and not be taken up with trifles, and this will put life into our endeavours. It is for a glorious and blessed estate on which we employ all this labour.[6]

This is the positive side of purification!

In the church today, we have underemphasized the future motivation (i.e., our Christian hope) for how to live the sanctified life. As with the Lord's Supper, we do not only look back to Christ's death but also look now to the risen Christ and forward to the future blessings that await us. This is the purification of the truly hopeful.

Part 3

LOVE

Question 31

What is the foundation of
the Christian religion?

The foundation of the Christian religion is
the love of God toward his people through
Christ and the love of his people for him.

The great mark of the Christian faith—if we have to pick one—
is love. Christians are to "owe no one anything, except to love each
other, for the one who loves another has fulfilled the law" (Rom.
13:8). Jesus declared to his disciples, "A new commandment I give
to you, that you love one another: just as I have loved you, you also
are to love one another. By this all people will know that you are
my disciples, if you have love for one another" (John 13:34–35).
But to understand Christian love, we must go back further, to the
eternal God of love.

Love binds God to his people. There can be no stronger bond,
for it finds its basis in the bond of love existing between the three
persons of the Trinity. Thus, when we are bound to God in love,
we share in the life of the triune God. Remove love from our

149

relationship to him, and we become the most miserable of all creatures. Faith and hope cry out for love as a newborn cries out for milk.

Love exists as the foundation of the Christian religion because our salvation arises out of God's love in Christ: "In love he predestined us for adoption to himself as sons through Jesus Christ, according to the purpose of his will" (Eph. 1:4–5). Paul here addresses the eternal basis for our present hope and salvation. As Geerhardus Vos notes, "The reason God will never stop loving you is that he never began."[1] This being the case, even before the fall necessitated the sacrifice of Christ, God out of condescending love determined to have a people for himself. Based on Jeremiah 31:3 ("I have loved you with an everlasting love"), we may be assured, as Vos explains, that God will never cease to love us because he has always loved us. But we may also say that God must necessarily love us forever because he must necessarily love his Son forever. To love Christ is to love us, and vice versa.

Once we go back to God's love as the foundation for our salvation in Christ, we can go back no further. In this manner, we must recognize that he loved us not because Christ died for us but simply because he loved us. His love for us explains all that he did for us and will do for us. Our faith and hope look forward to the eternal bounties of his love.

Charles Spurgeon speaks of the importance of love coming down to us from God through Christ:

As love comes from heaven, so it must feed on heavenly bread. It cannot exist in this wilderness, unless it is nurtured from above, and fed by manna from on high. On what, then, does love feed? Why, it feeds on love. That which brought it forth becomes its food. "We love him because he first loved us." The constant motive and sustaining power of our love to God is his love to us.[2]

Martin Luther describes the idea of God's love "finding us out" in his Heidelberg Disputation of 1518. There he makes some vital points concerning the love of God, which he says "does not find, but creates, that which is pleasing to it," in contrast to the love of man, which "comes into being through that which is pleasing to it."[3] Humans respond to God's love. He has made us in his image so that we love that which is lovable. Yet his love does not quite work in this way. He does not "answer" as we do to something attractive, but his love creates something attractive. As Luther observes,

> God . . . loves sinners, evil persons, fools, and weaklings in order to make them righteous, good, wise, and strong. Rather than seeking its own good, the love of God flows forth and bestows good. Therefore sinners are attractive because they are loved; they are not loved because they are attractive.[4]

While our love for God differs in significant respects from God's love for us, our love for him remains the goal of his love for us. Augustine understood well the necessity that love for God arise out of his love for us: "All who do not love God are strangers and antichrists. They might come to the churches, but they cannot be numbered among the children of God. That fountain of life does not belong to them."[5] He was, of course, merely echoing the apostle Paul, who ended his letter to the Corinthians, "If anyone has no love for the Lord, let him be accursed" (1 Cor. 16:22).

As Christians, we do well to ask, what does God want from us? He desires that we love him and his Son, Jesus Christ. For we are never more like our heavenly Father than when we love the Son. Christ is the principal object of the Father's love; the Father is the principal object of Christ's love. The Holy Spirit binds them together in an eternally loving relationship whereby the eternal state of blessedness will simply flow from the reality of this loving relationship. No wonder, then, that Christ was so concerned that his disciples should love him. Hence his three questions to Peter:

Simon, son of John, do you love me more than these? (John 21:15)

Simon, son of John, do you love me? (John 21:16)

Simon, son of John, do you love me? (John 21:17)

We might be tempted to think that these questions were purely for Peter's sake, namely, that he might have occasion to testify that he really did love his Savior, despite his threefold disowning of Christ. But surely we stand on solid ground in maintaining that Christ, who remains fully human, desires that his sheep express their love for him. In other words, Christ would not be truly human if he did not care about and delight in the love his children have for him.

Love for Christ is obvious, extravagant, and ultimately "unaware." Consider Christ's words about the sinful woman in contrast to Simon the Pharisee in Luke 7:44–46:

Then turning toward the woman he said to Simon, "Do you see this woman? I entered your house; you gave me no water for my feet, but she has wet my feet with her tears and wiped them with her hair. You gave me no kiss, but from the time I came in she has not ceased to kiss my feet. You did not anoint my head with oil, but she has anointed my feet with ointment."

What this woman showed to Christ was nothing less than the outpouring of the love in her soul for someone who deserved nothing less. She was "unaware" in the sense that she was unconcerned with what all those around her except for Christ thought of her actions. Her love was filled with extravagance, as love should be when it reaches its zenith toward God and Christ.

When we love someone with true love, we not only love the person, but we also love our loving of the person. True love, as in the case of this woman, loves the loving of her Savior. We love loving Christ. Love for Christ is true virtue; as such, we can love without uncertainty and can have confidence in our love. Love for Christ cannot disappoint us, even if it is imperfect love, because imperfect love can still be true love.

Those of us who have sung Isaac Watts's glorious hymn "When I Survey the Wondrous Cross" (1707) are privileged to confess our love: "Love so amazing, so divine, demands my soul, my life, my all." Why? Because of Christ's amazing and divine love to give his soul, his life, his all. His love of greatest intensity demands the most passionate love from us in response. Consider Anselm of Canterbury's prayer on this matter:

> My God,
> I pray that I may so know you and love you
> that I may rejoice in you.
> And if I may not do so fully in this life
> let me go steadily on
> to the day when I come to that fullness. . . .
>
> Meanwhile let my mind meditate on it
> let my heart love it
> let my mouth preach it
> let my soul hunger for it
> my flesh thirst for it
> and my whole being desire it
> until I enter into the joy of my Lord.[6]

Question 32

What is love?

Love is a virtue that seeks union,
satisfaction, and goodwill.

Love remains difficult to define. Paul speaks of love as the most excellent way in 1 Corinthians 13 and describes love as keeping the commandments in Romans 13:8–10. The Ten Commandments represent the guide for how Christians can show their love toward God and others. Such love involves the whole person: "Hear, O Israel: The LORD our God, the LORD is one. You shall love the LORD your God with all your heart and with all your soul and with all your might" (Deut. 6:4–5). Love, however, must also be described in a way that may be true not only of our love for God but also of his love for us.

Love is a virtue whereby we praise God as the chief good. Love must be regarded as an act of worship, since the latter proceeds from the former. Because we possess faith and hope as virtues, we understand the goodness of God and cannot help but respond to him in love. Peter Lombard claims that "charity is the love by which God is loved for his own sake, and our neighbor is loved for the sake of God or in God."[1] Ultimately, all true love has God as its object, even if that love is shown "horizontally" (i.e., to our neighbor).

Love for God necessitates knowledge of him. We must believe that God exists and trust in him, through Christ, in order to love him. Faith, logically speaking, precedes love. In his wonderful analysis of love, William Ames says,

> Therefore, not love but faith is the first foundation of the spiritual building of man. This is so not only because faith is the beginning, but also because it sustains and holds together all the parts of the building. It has the nature of a root in that it gives power to bring forth fruit.[2]

Love leads to a "love of union, of satisfaction or contentment, and good will"—Ames calls these the "parts of love."[3] These "parts of love" are not one-way (i.e., from us to God) but are in fact two-way (i.e., God to us and us to God). Three constituent parts explain the goal of love from God to us and us to God:

1. The love of union: We desire to be with God through union with Christ. God desires union with his people. He accomplishes this union through his Son, which is the greatest spiritual blessing we possess. By hoping for and believing in good things from God, we love him for who he is to us. For this reason, God remains the highest end of our love.
2. The love of satisfaction: We desire to know who God is. His attributes—all of them—satisfy us, because knowledge of his being is the chief source of our joy, blessedness, and glory. God is also satisfied in us, for he delights in the good in us, which ultimately comes from him. He cannot but love those gifts that he himself gives to us.
3. The love of goodwill: We devote ourselves entirely to God by yielding to him in all things. All glory, honor, and praise are due to him. He exhibits goodwill toward his people as

well. He grants to us good things because he loves us. We cannot grant any good thing to him who is infinitely good and in need of nothing, but we can and must acknowledge his goodness because of who he is.[4]

The love we have for God, but more importantly, that which he has for us, involves union, satisfaction, and goodwill. In terms of our love for him, Ames discusses three additional marks that clarify its nature:

First, *objectively* (as they say)—because of the nature of the object, for whom we should desire greater good than for any other. Second, *appreciatively* (as some say)—because of our esteem, seen in our preference for him and his will above all other things, even our life, Matt. 10:37; Luke 14:26. Thus we should choose to die rather than to transgress even the least of his commandments. Third, *intensively*—all the faculties being fervently applied to loving God (Deut. 6:5).[5]

We love God objectively, appreciatively, and intensively.

It must be said that we cannot give our neighbors this type of love, since they are not the ultimate goal of our love. Still, this leaves our neighbors in a better position, as it assures them that our love for them finds its basis in something greater than them. Those who do not love God in this manner do not desire to be with him (i.e., in union). Thus, they end up receiving in hell what they desired on earth. The wicked see nothing delightful in God and have no goodwill toward him. Instead, the wicked have an inordinate love of themselves, which, incidentally, is a form of self-hate.

Since we see God in the face of Jesus Christ, our desire for union and communion (i.e., satisfaction and goodwill) with Christ remains the surest sign of our love for union and communion with God. Thus, Christ says, "Whoever hates me hates my Father also" (John 15:23). And in his High Priestly Prayer, Christ explains what constitutes eternal life: "And this is eternal life, that they know you, the only true God, and Jesus Christ whom you have sent" (John 17:3). We thus seek union, satisfaction, and goodwill with God and Christ through the power of the Spirit.

Jonathan Edwards makes the essential point that Christian love comes from the Spirit: "The Spirit of God is a Spirit of love, and when the former enters the soul, love also enters with it. God is love, and he that has God dwelling in him by his Spirit, will have love dwelling in him also."[6] Thus, there is something truly supernatural in the love between God and his people: God loves us, and we, by the Spirit, love him.

Question 33

What is the guide to loving God and our neighbor?

The Ten Commandments are the guide
to loving God and our neighbor.

"Love is a sweet word, but sweeter the deed," said Augustine.[1] Ultimately, the good deed matters most. But how do we know what these good deeds are or how they are to be done? God has not left us in ignorance but has given his Ten Commandments, which are a rule of conduct for all people, whether Adam in the garden, Moses in the wilderness, Christ on earth, or us today.

God gave the Ten Commandments at Mount Sinai as a rule for his newly constituted people, the nation of Israel. They provide a summary of his moral law and are addressed to the people settling in the Promised Land. With the failure of his people to abide by that law and the success of Christ in fulfilling it, the question remains whether these laws remain the obligation of the church, whose constitution transcends all geopolitical boundaries. Even among those who see an organic connection between the old- and new-covenant people of God, some wonder whether the church in the gospel era falls under the demands of the Ten Commandments.

Thus, the church has discussed and debated at length the ongoing application of the Ten Commandments (Ex. 20:1–17). Certain statements in the New Testament seem to cast a negative light on the law, while others speak of it more positively. If we understand the termination of the law in a redemptive-historical context, some of the problems begin to disappear. In other words, being *under* grace, we are no longer *under* the law in one sense but are in another (Rom. 6:14–15). If we fail to recognize this context, we will end up pitting certain texts (e.g., 2 Corinthians 3; Rom. 6:14; 7:5–6; Galatians 3–4) against others (e.g., Rom. 8:4; 13:8–10; 1 Cor. 7:19).

In Paul's writings, "law" usually refers to the law given at Sinai. For Israelites, the law was all or nothing.[2] There are "shifting elements" around an "unchanging core." The "unchanging core" is the moral element of the Ten Commandments. In other words, law abides not only before Moses (Gen. 26:5) but also after Christ (Rom. 13:8–10).

Some scholars reject the so-called threefold division of the law, namely, its moral, ceremonial, and civil aspects. But the Decalogue (Ten Commandments) clearly takes a unique place in how God governs all men and so allows the distinction between moral and ceremonial. God delivered the Ten Commandments to the Israelite congregation (Deut. 4:12–13) on stone tablets (Deut. 5:22) by the finger of God (Ex. 31:18) and for preservation in the ark (Deut. 10:1–5). Conversely, the civil laws came from Moses, not directly from God (Deut. 4:14), and were for a people constituting themselves in the Promised Land alone (Deut. 5:30–6:1).[3] Scripture also recognizes a distinction between the moral and ceremonial law (see Isa. 1:11–17; Matt. 23:23).

Thus, when Paul speaks "negatively" about the law, he discusses it in its redemptive-historical function and not in its unchanging rule in the Christian life. For example, in Galatians 3:24–25, Paul writes, "So then, the law was our guardian until Christ came, in order that we might be justified by faith. But now that faith has come, we are no longer under a guardian." The guardian of the "law" refers to the entirety of the old covenant, including the types and shadows. Thus God's covenant history with his people, "Israel," looks like this:

1. Promise (Abraham)
2. Law (Moses)
3. Fulfillment (Christ and the Spirit)

The promise (Abraham) comes as a future indicative regarding what God will do for his people and is ultimately fulfilled in Christ. The law (Moses) gets declared as a present imperative for the Israelites under the rule of God. The fulfillment (Christ and the Spirit) emerges as a present indicative for the church.

Why, then, does Paul sometimes speak "negatively" about the law in the New Testament? He speaks this way because the law in Moses's time awaited the indicative (i.e., Christ's work), which was still future. The indicative for the Israelites was merely typological (cf. Ex. 20:2; Rom. 6:15–23). From the Israelites' perspective, the great promises of the coming Messiah awaited fulfillment.

Now that Christ has come, the imperatives (i.e., commands) come to us in a different context from ancient Israel, when they received the law with the Ten Commandments. The law now more than ever has stability in the lives of God's people because we obey out of the grand realities of Christ's finished work. Redemption has been accomplished! So when we come to the New Testament, we indeed find many references to the positive side of keeping God's law. For example, 1 Timothy 1:8–11 gives us what might be most of the Decalogue:

Now we know that the law is good, if one uses it lawfully, understanding this, that the law is not laid down for the just but for the lawless and disobedient, for the ungodly and sinners, for the unholy and profane, for those who strike their fathers and mothers, for murderers, the sexually immoral, men who practice homosexuality, enslavers, liars, perjurers, and whatever else is contrary to sound doctrine, in accordance with the gospel of the glory of the blessed God with which I have been entrusted.

We can highlight the following parallels:

- fourth commandment: "unholy and profane" (v. 9; the Sabbath was a "holy" day)
- fifth commandment: "those who strike their fathers and mothers" (v. 9)
- sixth commandment: "murderers" (v. 9)
- seventh commandment: "the sexually immoral" (v. 10)
- eighth commandment: "enslavers" (v. 10)
- ninth commandment: "liars, perjurers" (v. 10)

In other places, Paul writes commands to Christians that are given in the same form in which Moses delivered God's commandments to the Israelites. Paul offers a general application of God's law in Galatians 5:14, "For the whole law is fulfilled in one word: 'You shall love your neighbor as yourself.'" But he also gives specific applications of God's law in other places. For example, in Romans 13:8–10, we read:

Owe no one anything, except to love each other, for the one who loves another has fulfilled the law. For the commandments, "You shall not commit adultery, You shall not murder, You shall not steal, You shall not covet," and any other commandment, are summed up in this word: "You shall love your neighbor as yourself." Love does no wrong to a neighbor; therefore love is the fulfilling of the law.

Or consider Ephesians 6:2–3: "'Honor your father and mother' (this is the first commandment with a promise), 'that it may go well with you and that you may live long in the land.'"

Notice that in both Romans 13:9 and Ephesians 6:2–3, Paul is applying the law to Christians in its Decalogue form. But in Romans 13, he does not see an antithesis between "law" and "love"; rather, the way to love is by keeping the law. Moreover, there are roughly fourteen quotations and twelve verbal allusions in the New Testament that come from the Ten Commandments in Exodus 20:1–17. Largely, they are used "positively" in the sense of the type of behavior expected of Christians in the new covenant.

We do not, then, believe that God's commandments are replaced by love. Rather, love fulfills the commandments. The law is a law of love, expressed in delight (love) for the law, which guides us in our love. Christians should be glad that we are given specific instructions in how to love. These imperatives in the New Testament all find their basis in the moral law that came in the form of the Ten Commandments to Israel.

Question 34

How do we fail to show love for God?

We fail to show love for God by
breaking his commandments.

In the beginning, God required Adam to keep his commandments as an expression of love for God. Adam ended up breaking all Ten Commandments, written not yet on tablets of stone but already on his heart. By eating from the forbidden tree, he acted in hatred and wicked self-love (Gen. 2:16–17; 3:6). He sinned, and such is lawlessness (1 John 3:4).

William Ames speaks of the ways men ascend to ungodliness and hatred of God:

> First, sinners have an inordinate love of themselves. Second, they will what they please, although it is contrary to the law of God. Third, they hate the law because it is contrary to their desire. Fourth, they oppose God himself who is the giver and author of such law.[1]

Self-love springs from unbelief as the hateful reaction to a loving God. Man's unbelief, distrust, pride, and presumption are all antithetical to the first commandment, which calls for exclusive worship of the true and living God (Ex. 20:3).

Adam also broke the other commandments. Regarding the second commandment, God defines acceptable worship as that occurring with "clean hands and a pure heart" (Ps. 24:4). But God also delineates the manner in which we must worship him. Adam showed self-love by failing to worship God appropriately in his sanctuary. Instead, Adam tolerated false religion. As God's prophet, priest, and king, Adam should have guarded the temple of God from evil intruders and imposters. Crushing the head of the Serpent was his responsibility. Consequently, Christ took up the task of Serpent bruiser (Gen. 3:15).

Regarding the third commandment, Adam disgraced the name of God. As his son and image bearer, Adam brought dishonor on his Father, failing to give him the preeminence he deserves. When God spoke to him and warned him, Adam was under obligation, according to the third commandment, to reverently use and apply God's Word. In waging war against the Serpent, Adam should have testified to the truth as God's chief representative.

Regarding the fourth commandment, Adam trampled God's eternal Sabbath rest. He was expected, as are we, to make every effort to enter God's rest (Heb. 4:11). He failed to worship and "rest" in God when he allowed his wife to eat from the forbidden tree. He jeopardized his eternal rest, in violation of the Sabbath. Here was a true lack of holy self-love and love for his wife, future children, and future grandchildren, since he jeopardized their Sabbath rest.

Regarding the fifth commandment, Adam failed to honor his Father. He would have had "long days" if he had done so. Instead, he died under a curse because he failed to love God.

Regarding the sixth commandment, Adam became a murderer by bringing death through sin to his posterity. He acted like the Devil by rejecting life through his sin against God (see Rom. 5:12–21).

He had a duty to provide life to his posterity, but he gave them death instead.

Regarding the seventh commandment, Adam showed unfaithfulness when he did not stop his wife from speaking with the Devil. He should have protected Eve, but he did not. In failing to love his wife, he broke the seventh commandment. Again, a failure to keep the seventh commandment was a failure to love.

Regarding the eighth commandment, Adam allowed his wife to steal. She took what was not hers to take. He also joined in the act of theft.

Regarding the ninth commandment, he became like the Father of Lies (John 8:44) by failing to speak the truth about God. Adam questioned and did not uphold God's goodness. Adam should have confronted Satan's slander. He allowed a lie to be perpetuated by letting Eve take the forbidden fruit.

Regarding the tenth commandment, Adam was discontent with his estate. He failed to find happiness in what God had given him. Adam coveted that which God had forbidden.

The above explains why Adam's apostasy from God was so evil. He did not merely make a mistake but willfully sinned against God and his neighbor. In his unbelief, he thus broke all of God's commandments, not just one. Fundamentally, his faith working through love should have kept him from sinning. Where love is absent, disobedience is present. As Adam loved God, he would necessarily have kept his commandments. The fall, then, was a departure from God—a hateful withdrawal from a loving God.

People are at enmity with God (Rom. 8:7). Hostility exists in everyone, whether sinner or saint, and it wages war against God and his commandments. In one respect, the sins of the unconverted are worse because they never lead to true remorse. Christians usually sin with remorse because of the Spirit who dwells in them (Rom. 8:9). In another respect, the sins of Christians are worse because, compared to unbelievers, they sin with both greater knowledge of evil and greater power to resist.

Breaking God's commandments—something his children still do—shows that we still sometimes rebel. These violations are never a matter of simply "breaking rules" but rather a sign of disdain for God himself. Because of indwelling sin, we love to abstract God's commandments from him so as to lessen the heinousness of our sin. But however convenient this may be, we are deluding ourselves. Failing to love our neighbor is a failure to love God himself.

Question 35

How do we show our love for God?

As Christ did before us, we show our love
for God by keeping his commandments.

The Son of God showed his love for his Father by keeping his commandments.[1] In John 15:10, Christ informs his disciples that there is a connection between loving God and keeping his commandments: "If you keep my commandments, you will abide in my love, just as I have kept my Father's commandments and abide in his love." Elsewhere, our Lord says, "Whoever has my commandments and keeps them, he it is who loves me. And he who loves me will be loved by my Father, and I will love him and manifest myself to him" (John 14:21). As Ames observes, "An implicit part of charity is the keeping and fulfilling of all the commandments of God, Rom. 3:10; 1 John 2:5; 3:18. For he cannot truly love God who does not strive to please him in all things and to be like him."[2]

The first Adam broke God's commandments in the garden of Eden. But the last Adam, Christ Jesus, kept them in the wilderness under far more difficult circumstances. This does not even take into account that Christ lived perfectly under the demands of the ceremonial law as well.

No one has ever loved God like the Lord Jesus, who did so with all his heart, soul, strength, and mind. Jesus kept God's commandments because he loved him: "I do as the Father has commanded me, so that the world may know that I love the Father" (John 14:31). His whole life was a life of love and therefore of obedience. Love and obedience are not enemies but friends, especially in Christ's life, who obeyed first for himself (that he might please God and do so joyfully) and second for us (that his obedience might one day be ours by gratuitous imputation). Jesus willingly and joyfully kept all the Ten Commandments.

Regarding the first commandment, Jesus worshiped and glorified God truly and exclusively while on earth (John 17:4). He feared, believed, and trusted his Father (Luke 4:1–12; Heb. 2:13; 5:7). He showed zeal for the Father's glory (John 2:17) and thanked him constantly (John 11:41). He yielded complete obedience to him in all things (John 10:17; 15:10). He refused to render glory, worship, or obedience to any other, as so powerfully manifested during his time of temptation (Matt. 4:1–11).

Regarding the second commandment, Jesus worshiped God faithfully, purely, and comprehensively. No one ever worshiped God like Christ did (Luke 4:16). Regarding individual and organized worship, Jesus only taught, observed, and conducted such as God instructed (e.g., Matt. 6:1–18). He read, preached, prayed, and sang God's Word with a pure heart (Ps. 24:3–4). He condemned false worship (Matt. 15:9; John 4:22), and as the visible image of God, he made no unlawful images of him.

Regarding the third commandment, Jesus never took God's name in vain. As his image bearer (Col. 1:15), Jesus perfectly revealed the Father (John 14:9) and declared only the words the Father gave him (John 12:49). Jesus spoke of God and his Word only in a holy and reverent manner and never lightly or profanely (e.g., Matt. 4:1–11).

Regarding the fourth commandment, Jesus faithfully kept God's day of Sabbath rest: "As was his custom, he went to the synagogue on the Sabbath day" (Luke 4:16). He did works of piety, mercy, and necessity on the Sabbath (e.g., Mark 2:23–28). As one who corrected the distortions of men regarding the Sabbath made for them, he showed himself to be "lord of the Sabbath" (Matt. 12:8). As such, he secured our eternal Sabbath rest (Heb. 4:6–9) by dying on the cross, resting in the grave on the Sabbath, and rising on the Lord 's Day.

Regarding the fifth commandment, Jesus did only that which pleased his heavenly Father (John 8:29), and the Father confirmed such faithfulness before the world (Matt. 3:17). On the cross, even as he was dying, Jesus took care of his mother (John 19:27). He also kept the laws of the land (Matt. 17:24–27; Mark 12:17).

Regarding the sixth commandment, Jesus preserved and gave life. He did so both physically and spiritually. He saved sinners (Luke 19:10) and healed many (Matt. 4:23). On earth, he showed meekness, gentleness, kindness, and peace (e.g., Matt. 11:29). His life was one of mercy and compassion (e.g., Luke 18:35–43). While he will come in the future on a "white horse," making war to "strike down" the wicked (Rev. 19:11, 15), Jesus can never be accused of murder. He remains the most just of judges.

Regarding the seventh commandment, Christ, as our faithful husband, laid down his life for his bride and continues to faithfully sanctify and prepare her for himself alone (Eph. 5:22–33). While Jesus would have recognized the beauty of women, he never lusted or behaved unseemly toward them. In the end, his thoughts were always pure toward the opposite sex (cf. 1 Tim. 5:2).

Regarding the eighth commandment, Christ gave freely (John 2:1–11), never took anything that did not belong to him or that was unjustly offered (Matt. 4:1–11), and opposed robbery (John 2:13–17). John 2 has in view, among other things, Christ's obedience to the eighth commandment. Instead of greedily grasping for the things of this world, he freely gave all that he possessed. The one who was rich became poor so that we, in our poverty, might become rich (2 Cor. 8:9).

Regarding the ninth commandment, Jesus always spoke the truth (John 8:45–47), because he only declared what the Father gave him (John 12:49). He stood for the truth as the Truth (John 1:14, 17; 14:6). He did not flatter (Matthew 23) or speak the truth unseasonably or in a concealed way (Matt. 26:64).

Regarding the tenth commandment, Jesus did not covet that which was not rightly his but received his inheritance by patiently enduring the cross. The one who owns heaven and earth said, "Foxes have holes, and birds of the air have nests, but the Son of Man has nowhere to lay his head" (Luke 9:58). The one who could have easily supplied his every need and desire instead received that which came from the Father's hand (Luke 4:1–12).

Reformed preaching must do a better job of explaining how Christ perfectly kept the law. It is one thing to say over and over again, "Jesus kept the law perfectly for us [as a covenant of works] so that we could be saved." But it is another thing to explain precisely how he kept the law. Christ's active obedience and God's imputation of that active obedience to us through faith should never be reduced to mere pithy statements.

In union with Christ, we follow in the pattern of our Savior. We keep God's commandments not so that he will love us but because he loves us and we him. We can speak all we want about our love for God, but it must be shown in action: "Let us not love in word or talk but in deed and in truth" (1 John 3:18). As John also says, "For this is the love of God, that we keep his commandments. And his commandments are not burdensome" (1 John 5:3).

Indeed, nothing fundamentally has changed over time in what God desires from us:

> And now, Israel, what does the LORD your God require of you, but to fear the LORD your God, to walk in all his ways, to love him, to serve the LORD your God with all your heart and with all your soul, and to keep the commandments and statutes of the LORD, which I am commanding you today for your good? (Deut. 10:12–13)

Question 36

What makes our obedience acceptable to God?

Obedience becomes acceptable to God when it is worked by the Spirit and motivated by love.

"The fruit of the Spirit is love . . ." (Gal. 5:22). Christ, through the Spirit, is in believers (Rom. 8:9–10), in order that believers may have the strength to obey God from the root of love. After all, Christianity has always been a religion that demands love from the heart (Deut. 6:5; Matt. 22:37). In a sermon on love from 1 John 4:4–12, Augustine claims,

> A bad person can receive the sacrament of the body and blood of the Lord. A bad person can have the name of Christ and be called a Christian. Such people are referred to when it says, "They polluted the name of their God" [Ezek. 36:20]. To have all these sacraments is, as I say, possible even for a bad person. But to have love and be a bad person is impossible. Love is the unique gift, the fountain that is yours alone. The Spirit of God exhorts you to drink from it, and in so doing to drink from himself.[1]

We may rightly argue that there is very little that a hypocrite cannot possess externally in the church compared to the true believer. A hypocrite may attend church, take the Lord's Supper, tithe, sing, pray, and so forth. But he cannot love because he cannot possess the Spirit of Christ and so does not belong to Christ (Rom. 8:8–9). As a result, hypocritical actions stem from a principle of something other than the love of Christ. As Augustine says in the same sermon, the root of love determines the actions of the Christian:

> A father beats a boy, while a kidnapper caresses him. Offered a choice between blows and caresses, who would not choose the caresses and avoid the blows? But when you consider the people who give them you realize that it is love that beats, wickedness that caresses. This is what I insist upon: human actions can only be understood by their root in love. All kinds of actions might appear good without proceeding from the root of love. Remember, thorns also have flowers: some actions seem truly savage, but are done for the sake of discipline motivated by love. Once and for all, I give you this one short command: love God, and do what you will.[2]

The last seven words of this quotation, spoken by the bishop of Hippo, have been rightly immortalized in the annals of church history. But the preceding words are equally profound. The Spirit necessarily produces loving actions in us, even if they appear to the ignorant or misinformed to be something other than love. God cares about the heart because that is where he dwells (1 John 4:12).

Actions that please God are those done in the power of the Spirit and in faith—for whatever is not of faith is sin (Rom. 14:23). God cannot be displeased with his own work in us. That is, the Father cannot reject the work of the Son or the work of the Spirit. God cannot reject himself.

Union with Christ (Gal. 2:20), which entitles us to the possession of the Spirit of Christ, means that we are in a position to please God. Paul says we can please God (Rom. 14:18; Phil. 4:18; 1 Thess. 4:1; Heb. 13:21). But we can also please Christ (2 Cor. 5:9). Though indwelling sin remains a present reality for all of God's people, our obedience may be described as "fully pleasing" to Christ (Col. 1:10).

The Christian life is filled with many setbacks, disappointments, failings, and heartaches, but that does not mean Christians are defeated. We are more than conquerors because of God's love (Rom. 8:37). In our battle, we cannot adopt the attitude that our love to God is meaningless to him. Rather, out of his abundant grace, he tells us that our imperfect love is pleasing to him.

God loves our love because all love comes from him and all love should be directed to him. But all actions pleasing to God must spring from love. Otherwise, our obedience cannot please God. John exhorts his readers to love one another, "for love is from God, and whoever loves has been born of God and knows God" (1 John 4:7). If a person does not love, then he or she cannot claim to know God, "because God is love" (1 John 4:8). The stakes are that high. For a Christian to lack love is nothing less than to lack Christ himself.

Is not this principle at the heart of Paul's magnificent words on love to the Corinthians? We can "speak in the tongues of men and of angels," but if we do not have love, then we are a "clanging cymbal" (1 Cor. 13:1). We can give away all that we possess, but if there is no root of love in such gifts, then we have gained nothing (1 Cor. 13:3). If there is no principle of love in our actions, God cannot and will not be pleased.

Question 37

How does faith work through love?

Faith works through love by keeping
the commandments of God.

In Galatians 5:6, Paul speaks of "faith working through love."
Faith and love are not identical. Rather, love exists as the fruit of
true, saving faith. In another place, Paul speaks to the works produced by faith: "To this end we always pray for you, that our God
may make you worthy of his calling and may fulfill every resolve
for good and every work of faith by his power" (2 Thess. 1:11).
The power comes from God, but our faith remains active as God
brings our works to fulfillment.

   We must distinguish faith and love, but they are inseparably joined
together. Faith does not justify through love, and faith is not acceptable on the basis of love. But faith does "work" and is not stagnant.
Just as God cannot give us justification without sanctification (1 Cor.
1:30), so he cannot give us the gift of faith without it producing acts of
love. According to William Ames, faith works through love "not because the whole effectiveness of faith depends upon love as a cause but
because faith manifests and exercises its power by stirring up love."[1]

175

So while faith is the "alone instrument of justification" (WCF 11.2), we also insist that it is "not alone in the person justified, but is ever accompanied with all other saving graces, and is no dead faith, but works by love" (WCF 11.2, quoting Gal. 5:6). Thus, as Richard Gaffin has pointed out,

> Paul does not teach a "faith alone" position. . . . Rather, his is a "by faith alone" position. . . . The faith by which sinners are justified, as it unites them to Christ and so secures for them all the benefits of salvation that there are in him, perseveres to the end and in persevering is never alone. Faith is, as Luther is reported to have said, "a busy little thing."[2]

The above concept of "faith alone" remains contrary to the Protestant spirit, which sought to do justice to texts speaking gloriously of justification apart from works and "conditionally" of the necessary obedience in the life of the Christian (John 6:53; Rom. 8:13; Gal. 5:16–26). The "by faith alone" idea expresses justification more clearly and safely without abandoning the doctrine of sanctification.

In the history of Christian dogmatics, Protestant theologians have been keen to distinguish between faith and love. For example, John Calvin makes this salient point:

> We confess with Paul that no other faith justifies "but faith working through love" [Gal. 5:6]. But it does not take its power to justify from that working of love. Indeed, it justifies in no other way but in that it leads us into fellowship with the righteousness of Christ. Otherwise, everything that the apostle insists upon so vigorously would fall [see Rom. 4:4–5].[3]

But what does it actually mean for faith to work "through love"? Faith "works" in relation to love in the sense that it "responds" to God's commandments. Faith, in the life of the Christian, does not stand in opposition to the law of God. Anthony Burgess, a Westminster divine who wrote copiously on the doctrine of justification by faith alone, makes this point about the law in relation to the Christian:

> If the Law, and the commands thereof be impossible, to what purpose then does [God] command them? Why does he bid us turn to him when we cannot? Then we answer, that these commandments are not only informing of a duty, but they are practical and operative means appointed by God, to work, at least in some degree, that which is commanded.[4]

Burgess claims that the moral law becomes an "operative means" working, "in some degree, that which is commanded." The law, as the guide for how to love God and neighbor, exists as a true instrument of sanctification. Faith working through love cannot be understood apart from the moral law. Otherwise, we are left guessing as to what that looks like. In other words, what does it mean to love if love is not the specific commandment of God?

The law that Christ commends can be summarized in the following:

> You shall love the Lord your God with all your heart and with all your soul and with all your mind. This is the great and first commandment. And a second is like it: You shall love your neighbor as yourself. On these two commandments depend all the Law and the Prophets. (Matt. 22:37–40)

So before James refers to showing faith by works (James 2:18), he speaks of faith fulfilling the law: "If you really fulfill the royal law according to the Scripture, 'You shall love your neighbor as yourself,' you are doing well" (James 2:8). Faith working through love is to fulfill the "royal law" that James speaks of. Consider Paul's language to the Corinthians and the Galatians:

> For neither circumcision counts for anything nor uncircumcision, but keeping the commandments of God. (1 Cor. 7:19)

> For in Christ Jesus neither circumcision nor uncircumcision counts for anything, but only faith working through love. (Gal. 5:6)

> For neither circumcision counts for anything, nor uncircumcision, but a new creation. (Gal. 6:15)

This new-covenant "triad" of verses above connects obedience to faith and love in an organic way. In other words, believers are a new creation in Christ (2 Cor. 5:17) and are born into a living hope (1 Pet. 1:3) marked by faith working through love and realized by keeping God's commandments. Here we are faced with "mere" Christianity: new creatures walking by faith in obedience to God's commandments. This is how we declare our love to him as we patiently wait in hope for God to vindicate his people at the final day.

Faith working through love necessitates not simply a response to an outward commandment but also the internalizing of the law in the heart with a faith busy keeping God's commandments. So to "work through love" and to "keep God's commandments" are roughly synonymous concepts in Paul. Faith and love are not identical, just as faith and keeping God's commandments are not identical. Yet love and keeping God's commandments necessitate the principle of faith enabling us to "work."

Faith and the Spirit work together and conform us to the law made flesh (i.e., Christ). We look like Jesus because we keep his commandments. They show us how love looks. Accordingly, faith responds to God's commandments and gives us the ability to keep them because the Spirit takes them and writes them on our hearts.

Question 38

What is the context for our love?

We love in the context of the church both those
in the church and those outside the church.

To Cyprian (ca. 200–258) belongs the distinction of making well known the phrase "You cannot have God as your Father if you will not have the church as your mother."[1] But we find the truth expressed in a slightly different form in Augustine and others. For example, Calvin remarks,

> I shall start, then, with the church, into whose bosom God is pleased to gather his sons, not only that they may be nourished by her help and ministry as long as they are infants and children, but also that they may be guided by her motherly care until they mature and at last reach the goal of faith . . . so that, for those to whom he is Father the church may also be Mother. And this was so not only under the law but also after Christ's coming, as Paul testifies when he teaches that we are the children of the new and heavenly Jerusalem.[2]

The church of Jesus Christ, which he purchased with his own blood (Acts 20:28), exists as the context for our obedience. He could show no greater love to the church than laying down his life for his people (John 15:13). We must learn to love what Christ loves. His attitude toward the church sets the tone for our own attitude. If we do not love the church, then we hate the context in which love thrives. Any talk of obedience or love to God becomes meaningless without a proper context for expressing them.

For all the glorious truths of Paul in Ephesians, the letter makes no sense if we do not apply these truths to Christians in the context of the church. As part of Christ's ministry, he gifts to the church apostles, prophets, evangelists, shepherds, and teachers in order to "equip the saints for the work of ministry" (Eph. 4:12). These "gifts" help us, the body, to know Christ and grow into maturity as we avoid theological error. Importantly, Paul highlights the goal of our growth in knowledge in the church:

> Rather, speaking the truth in love, we are to grow up in every way into him who is the head, into Christ, from whom the whole body, joined and held together by every joint with which it is equipped, when each part is working properly, makes the body grow so that it builds itself up in love. (Eph. 4:15–16)

The church, through the teaching offered by Christ's ministers, must mature but always with the goal of achieving such in love. Growing in love, apart from the context of the church, remains foreign to the teaching of Scripture. As an infant grows through the nourishing milk of his or her mother, so we as spiritual "babes" grow through the church's nourishing teaching in order that we may be loving creatures.

Claiming to love adequately apart from the church despises Christ, who gifts the church. Its teachers must remind God's people that they must first receive from God before they can give to others, especially when it comes to love. The community of faith must hear that they cannot live the Christian life in isolation. In this way, elders are ordained to cultivate in the church an attitude of dependence on God. The elders and minister want their flock to depend not on them but on Christ.

Yet everyone in the church receives the call to stir up love and good works in others (Heb. 10:24). Thus, its members are called to exercise their graces among the weak, difficult, stubborn, and poor, all of whom God has drawn into the flock. Why receive the love of God in our hearts if we fail to return the same to others, even the most testing? After all, God loved us as the "difficult" ones so that we, within the church, might show the same to the "difficult."

C. S. Lewis, in his book *The Four Loves*, picks up on another aspect of love:

> To love at all is to be vulnerable. Love anything and your heart will be wrung and possibly broken. If you want to make sure of keeping it intact you must give it to no one, not even an animal. Wrap it carefully round with hobbies and little luxuries; avoid all entanglements. Lock it up safe in the casket or coffin of your selfishness. But in that casket, safe, dark, motionless, airless, it will change. It will not be broken; it will become unbreakable, impenetrable, irredeemable. To love is to be vulnerable.[3]

Love remains difficult not only because of whom we have to love but also because it makes us vulnerable. There is always the possibility that the love we show will not be returned. When you think that way, consider Christ's own life, in which he knew others would respond to his love with hatred. But that did not stop him from loving. In the end, love will ultimately win, no matter what the present may offer.

Moreover, we love those not only inside but also outside the church, even our enemies: "But I say to you, Love your enemies and pray for those who persecute you" (Matt. 5:44). Our adoption as children of God demands such an attitude (Matt. 5:45). Jonathan Edwards aptly notes,

> Love is the very temper and spirit of a Christian: it is the sum of Christianity. And if we consider what incitements thus to love our enemies we have set before us in what the Gospel reveals of the love of God and Christ to their enemies, we cannot wonder that we are required to love our enemies, and to bless them, and do good to them, and pray for them.[4]

We love in the context of the church, where we are taught how to love and whom to love. As the Scriptures teach, we are to do good to all, even our enemies, and especially to God's people (Gal. 6:10). We must not allow the command to love our enemies to be reduced to a nice yet ineffectual saying. It simply has to be done for our sake and for that of our enemies. They need our love, and we need to show it. Love to our enemies exists as our weapon against them, whether through kind words or prayers on their behalf. If the gospel has really taken root in our lives, we should remember that we were enemies of God and Christ, but yet they loved us. Their love won us, and our love can win our enemies. Loving our enemies requires patience, for their hearts are often subdued slowly, if at all. But love remains patient and kind, which puts our enemies at a massive disadvantage if they aim to remain hostile to us.

In the context of the church, as God's people, the world will know us by our sacrificial and self-giving love. As Christ said to his disciples, "A new commandment I give to you, that you love one another: just as I have loved you, you also are to love one another. By this all people will know that you are my disciples, if you have love for one another" (John 13:34–35).

Question 39

What is the chief end of our love to others?

The chief end of our love to others is to glorify God
and Christ by loving them first and foremost.

God comes first. David K. Naugle, making use of Augustine, rightly argues, "We love ourselves rightly when we love God more than ourselves, when he is our chief good. . . . We really don't love ourselves or anyone or anything else if we don't love God."[1] To love God first makes the most sense for us. Love of God restores our knowledge and lives, our affections and desires.

God is the beginning and the end, the eternally Majestic One. In terms of his own purposes in creation and redemption, God's "chief end" is the glory of himself and his Son, Jesus Christ. The Father accomplishes this by loving Christ. If our chief end is to glorify God and Christ, there is no doubt that we accomplish this the same way: through love. Love to God and love to our neighbor.

As Christians, our chief end is to glorify God the Father and Christ through the Spirit. In doing so, we will together enjoy our God forever (Rom. 11:36; 2 Cor. 13:14; Eph. 1:23; 3:16; Col. 1:16–18; Rev. 21:2). As we make the glory of God and Christ the goal of our love, we must remember that the Holy Spirit's principal role in redemption is to glorify Christ (John 16:14). By making us like Christ (2 Cor. 3:18), the Spirit glorifies Christ. The well-known question and answer at the beginning of the Westminster Shorter Catechism follows in this pattern:

Q. 1. What is the chief end of man?
A. Man's chief end is to glorify God, and to enjoy him forever.

God will be glorified, for it is impossible that he should not be glorified. But God will be glorified through love. The Son glorified the Father by loving us and giving himself up for us.

The Son loves us because the Father loved him. The flow of love begins from the Father to the Son through the Spirit and finds its way into our hearts because of Christ's work for us (John 15:9). We abide in Christ's love by keeping his commandments. Why? Because the pattern remains the same: Christ abides in his Father's love by keeping his commandments (John 15:10). Christ then says to his disciples, "This is my commandment, that you love one another as I have loved you. Greater love has no one than this, that someone lay down his life for his friends" (John 15:12–13).

If God is going to be glorified by his Son, then it will come through loving obedience. If we are going to glorify God and Christ, then it will come through loving obedience. William Ames rightly attests, "Theology is the doctrine or teaching of living to God. . . . Men live to God when they live in accord with the will of God, to the glory of God, and with God working in them."[2]

Whatever we do in this life must be to the aim of God's glory: "So, whether you eat or drink, or whatever you do, do all to the glory of God" (1 Cor. 10:31). Or consider Peter's words, ". . . whoever serves, as one who serves by the strength that God supplies—

in order that in everything God may be glorified through Jesus Christ. To him belong glory and dominion forever and ever. Amen" (1 Pet. 4:11).

Love gets wasted when it does not lead to God's glory. As Jonathan Edwards says, "Love to God will dispose a man to honour him, to worship and adore him, and heartily to acknowledge his greatness and glory and dominion."[3] Love is hatred when it has in view something other than God's glory. For our love to glorify God and Christ, we must give them preeminence in our lives, or we are playing a dangerous game—a very dangerous game indeed. We shall never enjoy glorifying God and Christ through love if we do not do so first and foremost for their sake.

A rich reward is promised to those who love: "Whoever has my commandments and keeps them, he it is who loves me. And he who loves me will be loved by my Father, and I will love him and manifest myself to him" (John 14:21). Jesus adds, "If anyone loves me, he will keep my word, and my Father will love him, and we will come to him and make our home with him" (John 14:23). Our love for Christ cannot go unrewarded. We are promised his intimate, covenantal presence when we love him in the context of keeping his commandments. Our duty can turn to delight if we meditate on this promise from the Savior, who wishes to dwell intimately with those who love him in return for all he has done on their behalf.

Question 40

How can we keep ourselves
from idolatry, which manifests
hatred toward God?

We keep ourselves from idolatry by worshiping the
triune God, which manifests our love toward him.

The apostle John commanded his readers to keep themselves from idols (1 John 5:21).[1] The negative side of the first commandment is to refrain from idolatry, since God is most displeased with idolatry among his people. But for every "negative" command (i.e., "do not"), we must keep in mind that there is a positive command.

The primary task of the church is not evangelism or good works to our neighbors, however important they may be, but the worship of the triune God, which necessarily manifests itself corporately. Corporate worship in the name of Christ by the power of the Spirit gives expression to our love.

In Christian worship, God the Father calls us into his presence. By the gift of the Holy Spirit, who binds us to Jesus, the Father brings us into heaven itself. Christian worship begins with the "downward" motion of God reaching out to us in love to grant us the gift of life. This "downward" motion is Trinitarian. Worship is made complete when we respond to God's grace with joyful thanksgiving and love of his majestic name.

There is Trinitarian activity in our response: by the gift of the Holy Spirit, we respond with faith, hope, and love to the Father's call in union with Christ. God created us to worship him, which is his prerogative as God (Ps. 95:6; Rev. 4:11; 14:7). We are at our best when we are worshiping the triune God; we are at our worst when we are worshiping anything or anyone else. Worship of God involves the whole person (Deut. 6:4–6).

In worship, we apply our hearts and minds to God's excellencies, to the thoughts of his attributes, such as his majesty and holiness (1 Chron. 16:29; Ps. 29:1–4). Our hearts embrace his goodness and enter into communion with him. The heart of the worshiper is an essential component of true worship, for multitudes honor God with their lips but not with their hearts (Isa. 29:13).

God demands worship from his creatures who are created in his image. But sin has perverted our worship and caused us to pursue that which is created rather the one who created it (Rom. 1:20–25). Hence, we need Christ to restore our relationship with God, since sin has alienated us from our Maker. Redemption in Christ restores our relationship. He alone can bridge the gap between God's holiness and our sin (1 Tim. 2:5), which he does by establishing a covenant relationship with us.

All knowledge of God, and so all worship of him, is rooted in this divine covenant (Pss. 25:14; 50:14–16). God begins this relationship, and we respond. He comes in love, and we respond in love. He comes in glory, and we respond in reverence (Heb. 12:28).

The centrality of Christ's mediation in the context of the covenant is a gift to the church, for we pray in his name, and priests are no longer necessary in the new covenant (Hebrews 8–9). While worship can take an individualistic form, the corporate aspect of worship dominates the pages of Scripture, particularly in the new covenant, where worship is almost exclusively so. This reflects the growing maturity of the church (i.e., Christ's body) and God's intention to have a treasured people for himself (Ex. 19:5–6; 1 Pet. 2:9).

The goal of evangelism is to be involved in gathering such a people from all nations to worship the Lord (Psalm 67; Isa. 2:2–4). As John Piper argues in relation to evangelism and the testimony of Psalm 67, "Missions exists because worship does not. Worship is ultimate, not missions, because God is ultimate, not man."[2] From the beginning, man had an obligation to hand himself over to God at a cost, and this obligation has only been increased by the penalties of sin. Worship in the divine covenant necessarily involves a sacrificial element (Gen. 4:3–5; 22; Leviticus 1), and this reaches its consummate expression in corporate worship.

The sacrificial offerings that were a major part of Israel's temple worship pointed the people to Christ, who was the fulfillment of what those sacrifices typified (Hebrews 9–10). In the new covenant, we approach God directly by Christ's sacrifice, and in union with Jesus, we become living sacrifices (Rom. 12:1) and offer spiritual sacrifices (Heb. 13:15–16; 1 Pet. 2:5).

On the Lord's Day, the corporate nature of worship reaches its zenith. Using the body analogy, Paul argues against a sort of "communism" where each person has the same role in worship. Each member is a particular part of the body and therefore performs a different function. True, all Christians are part of the royal priesthood (1 Pet. 2:9), but we minister differently according to the gifting of the Holy Spirit (1 Corinthians 12). Our worship consists not only of singing but also of listening, praying, and partaking of Communion.

Worship responds to God's acts and revelation in the Scriptures. For these reasons, worship must be in the power of the Spirit and according to truth (John 4:24). For Christians, that means that as we now, by faith, behold the glory of God in the face of Jesus Christ, we will be transformed into his likeness (2 Cor. 3:18; 4:6). Moreover, worship transcends time and place: though we are on earth, it is performed in heaven (Heb. 12:22–24).

The most important thing a Christian can do is worship God together with the body of Christ. We come together each Lord's Day as a unified army, fighting the Lord's battles in different ways, knowing that God is fighting with us and for us.

Worship is giving glory to God for his worth in the name of Jesus by the power of the Holy Spirit according to truth. We praise God, who gave to the church both his Son and his Spirit, for in giving these two persons, he had nothing left to give. In response to Christ's sacrifice, we become living sacrifices as we behold the glory of God in the face of Jesus Christ, who is the new temple and who draws all nations to himself (Isa. 2:2–3). This is our delight as Christians.

Question 41

What guards the church
from false worship?

The Bible alone as a sufficient rule for worshiping
God guards us from that which is false.

Godefridus Udemans correctly notes, "Spiritual worship involves
the exercise of true faith, hope, and love" (1 John 3:22–24).[1] As
we have seen throughout this book, our faith, hope, and love are
not ignorant but are based on knowledge coming from God's Word
through the Spirit.

Self-love, pride, and willful ignorance will let our imaginations
become a curse when we worship God. In ourselves, we simply are
not trustworthy enough to be able to determine how God ought
to be worshiped. Indeed, even in his state of innocence and righteousness, Adam received instructions from God concerning proper
worship.

There is such a thing as false worship, which the second commandment warns against. As Christ said to the Samaritan woman,
"You worship what you do not know; we worship what we know,

for salvation is from the Jews" (John 4:22). Salvation is connected to true worship (i.e., "what we know"). Of course, in the past, the Israelites had engaged in false worship, with painful consequences (Exodus 32; Lev. 10:1–3). They wandered from God's Word and commandments (see the warnings of Deut. 4:2; 12:32; 1 Sam. 15:22).

Instead, God's people are to reject pagan rites of worship: "They built the high places of Baal in the Valley of the Son of Hinnom, to offer up their sons and daughters to Molech, though I did not command them, nor did it enter into my mind, that they should do this abomination, to cause Judah to sin" (Jer. 32:35).

False worship assumes that there is such a thing as true worship: "But the hour is coming, and is now here, when the true worshipers will worship the Father in spirit and truth, for the Father is seeking such people to worship him. God is spirit, and those who worship him must worship in spirit and truth" (John 4:23–24). We must love God enough to joyfully and perpetually concede to him the right to dictate how he is best worshiped.

What does true worship look like? Without being too specific— since, as John Owen argues, we must allow Christians latitude in applying this principle—we can affirm some basic, valuable guidelines for the people of God. The Westminster Confession of Faith offers a succinct summary of what public worship should include:

> The reading of the Scriptures with godly fear; the sound preaching, and conscionable hearing of the Word, in obedience unto God with understanding, faith, and reverence; singing of psalms with grace in the heart; as, also, the due administration and worthy receiving of the sacraments instituted by Christ; are all parts of the ordinary religious worship of God. (21.5)

These elements of worship are designed to bring us into corporate communion with our triune God. Our faith, hope, and love are all strengthened when we respond to God in the manner he has ordained for the benefit of our souls.

If we claim to love God, we cannot detest the words that proceed from his mouth. One has to question how much we actually love God today, when man's words are more and more trumping God's in corporate worship. Our worship—whether our public prayers, hymns, or sermons—should be filled with God's Word and his truth.

It is one thing to claim that we are worshiping God in the way he has commanded but another thing entirely to actually do it. Our prayers ought to be suffused with God's Word. How many churches today regularly sing the Psalms, which are the very words of God? Some complain that so much contemporary worship is too emotional. I would argue that, in some sense, it is not emotional enough. By this I mean that much contemporary worship needs to lay aside the superficial feel-good approach in exchange for the range of emotions expressed in the Psalms that characterize the Christian life (e.g., lament, joy, thanksgiving, duress). What better way to express our love for God than to use the words he has inspired through those who have loved him?

If the first commandment highlights the fact that God alone has exclusive rights to our love, then the second commandment highlights, among many things, that our love as Christians must be pure toward its object (God). We cannot love ignorantly, because love requires truth (1 Cor. 13:6). This is nowhere more important than in the highest activity of humans—our worship of the triune God, who loves truthfully.

Question 42

How should God's people regard themselves in the Christian life?

God's people should regard themselves as his
image bearers in their conduct and speech,
whereby they hallow his name.

The manner in which we speak to God and of God reveals a great deal about our love for God. The third commandment tells us that we must "not take the name of the LORD [our] God in vain" (Ex. 20:7). Positively, that means we must hallow (i.e., keep holy or revere) his name. His name is already holy, and we can neither add anything to it nor take anything away from it. To hallow it means to set it apart or treat it as holy. We do this because we are his image bearers. Through baptism, we carry around the name Christian because we have put on Christ (Gal. 3:27). The stakes for us, then, are very high indeed since we are implicating our Savior, who dwells in our hearts through faith (Eph. 3:17), in all that we say and do.

Taking God's name as a child of God means we are to give him preeminence in all things. The issue between Cain and Abel was very simple: Abel's offering acknowledged God for who he is. In his view, nothing but the best was acceptable for God. That is why Abel's worship was approved and Cain's was not.

We are in the most dangerous position in the world when we claim God as our own but make him second to something else, in fact, another god. As his image bearers, we are made to worship him: "It is the LORD your God you shall fear. Him you shall serve and by his name you shall swear" (Deut. 6:13). Whatever we do in our lives, we do as his representatives.

You represent God in all you do in life, bearing his image in thought, speech, and action. Thus our conduct must be true to our image. If we are made in God's image, then we are to love the one in whose image we are made. Paul speaks of false teachers in the following way: "They profess to know God, but they deny him by their works. They are detestable, disobedient, unfit for any good work" (Titus 1:16). We cannot deny our God by committing unrelenting wicked acts, but instead, we must affirm him by living according to his will.

The first petition in the Lord's Prayer corresponds positively to the third commandment. "Hallowed be your name" should be a daily mantra of the Christian (Matt. 6:9). God's name is to be hallowed because his name is synonymous with his being. His name is also used synonymously with his redeeming work for sinners. Hence the following passages:

> And there is salvation in no one else, for there is no other name under heaven given among men by which we must be saved. (Acts 4:12)

> He sent redemption to his people;
> he has commanded his covenant forever.
> Holy and awesome is his name! (Ps. 111:9)

Not to us, O Lord, not to us, but to your name give glory,
  for the sake of your steadfast love and your faithfulness!
    (Ps. 115:1)

How do we hallow God's name? There are a number of ways we keep God's name holy, but these five are essential in the Christian life:

1. By loving his name: "But let all who take refuge in you rejoice; let them ever sing for joy, and spread your protection over them, that those who love your name may exult in you" (Ps. 5:11).
2. By trusting in his name: "Our soul waits for the Lord; he is our help and our shield. For our heart is glad in him, because we trust in his holy name" (Ps. 33:20–21).
3. By calling others to reverence and hallow the name of God: "I will bless the Lord at all times; his praise shall continually be in my mouth. My soul makes its boast in the Lord; let the humble hear and be glad. Oh, magnify the Lord with me, and let us exalt his name together!" (Ps. 34:1–3).
4. By blessing his name in the most difficult seasons: "The Lord gave, and the Lord has taken away; blessed be the name of the Lord" (Job 1:21).
5. By speaking the truth concerning God: "For I have not spoken on my own authority, but the Father who sent me has himself given me a commandment—what to say and what to speak. And I know that his commandment is eternal life. What I say, therefore, I say as the Father has told me" (John 12:49–50).

In order to appropriately love God in this life, we must first understand that in Christ we are his image bearers, and as such, our conduct and speech reflect directly on the God we serve. We have obligations to his name, and these obligations are the positive side of the third commandment, which tells us not to take his name in vain. So "Hallowed be your name" means, "Father, may your name be set apart in holiness by us as you set us apart unto yourself in sanctification."

Question 43

Does God offer us a particular day in which we may rest and stir up our love for him and others?

Yes, God has given us the Lord's Day, when the
church gathers to worship, as a unique day for
resting and stirring up our love for him and others.

God granted Adam one day out of seven in which he could take time to rest and meditate on God and his creation. This rest, built into the very fabric of creation by a good God who knows what is best for his creatures, was given to Israel. In the Ten Commandments, the Israelites are told the reason for their Sabbath resting: "For in six days the LORD made heaven and earth, the sea, and all that is in them, and rested on the seventh day. Therefore the LORD blessed the Sabbath day and made it holy" (Ex. 20:11).

Many argue that the Sabbath principle no longer remains active, now that we are under the new covenant. In the more sophisticated arguments against the continuation of the weekly

Sabbath, one finds the idea that we now rest in Christ, who is our Sabbath rest.

Whatever side a person falls on, we must recognize that God's rest in Genesis 2:2 ("And on the seventh day God finished his work that he had done, and he rested on the seventh day from all his work that he had done") remains a design and mandate for those made in his image to share in that rest. This verse is not simply descriptive of God but is also prescriptive for us.

Our resting on the Lord's Day in the new covenant is hugely significant. The eternal Sabbath rest still awaits us, for we have not yet entered into it (see Heb. 3:7–4:13). Our weekly resting on the Lord's Day serves as a sign of our corporate faith and hope that we will one day together enter the promised rest that awaits the people of God. In other words, resting on the Lord's Day is given to God's people on earth to stir up in them their faith, hope, and love.

The church is a pilgrim people in the wilderness, with the eternal rest promised to them in the future. But the one-day-in-seven principle, which now falls on the Lord's Day, is a way for us to focus our hearts and minds on what is to come for us who belong to Christ. If God's eternal rest still awaits his people, the day pointing to it, with the character of a Sabbath, still remains.

The goal of redemption is not to obliterate God's original purposes but in many ways to return his people to his original intention for them. The Israelites were given the law, including the Sabbath, in the context of the Promised Land. This redemption marks a sort of return to Eden. So the Sabbath is not merely a result of redemption; rather, it is a part of our redemption that brings us to God's intent for how his people should live. If Adam meditated restfully on God's works of creation during the Sabbath, then we in the new covenant not only meditate and rest likewise but also do so based on God's work of redemption.

Out of love, God gave humanity a divinely planned cycle of life.

In love toward Adam and his posterity, God gave us a day of rest. Instead of asking what we can and cannot do on the Lord's Day, perhaps Christians should first remember to thank God for building into creation the concept of rest. A day of rest is not something that is optional for us. We need it like we need air and water.

In the New Testament, we note that Christians began to live their lives according to the one-in-seven principle on the first day of the week, not the seventh day of the week (John 20:19; Acts 20:7; 1 Cor. 16:2). This day has the distinction of being called "the Lord's day" (Rev. 1:10), and it represents the dawning of a new era: the Lord of the Sabbath (Matt. 12:8) has inaugurated the new creation.

On the Lord's Day, we rest spiritually through works of mercy, necessity, and piety. In other words, the Lord's Day is a day to cultivate love for our neighbor. Whether in church, where we "consider how to stir up one another to love and good works" (Heb. 10:24), or in the community, where we show mercy to the needy, the Lord's Day is a day to love both God and our neighbor. One cannot help but think that perhaps many Christians, who are more concerned about what they cannot do than what they can do, have not adequately thought about the fact that the Lord's Day is a day for us to express our faith, hope, and love:

- Faith—that God will do his work in us through his appointed means of grace
- Hope—that God will bring us to our eternal rest where Christ awaits us
- Love—that God will stir up in us love for him and our neighbor

Thomas Watson highlights well the connection between meditating on the Lord's Day in relation to Christ's love: "How can we look on his bleeding and dying for us, and our hearts not be warmed with love to him? Love is the soul of religion, the purest affection. It is not rivers of oil, but sparks of love that Christ values."[1]

Returning to Genesis 2:2–3, we are reminded that the "rest" principle is not simply a command but also an invitation to participate in the very life of God. He created us in his image. Man and woman exist in the image of God, which means, in part, that we are to imitate God. We do as he does. He rests from his creation work, and he longs for us to join him in that rest. God has also rested from his redemptive work, and he longs for us to join him in that rest.

Because the Father has united us to Christ by the Spirit, we are able to enter that rest. God only requires of us what we already long to do because of our union with Christ. Because we no longer live but he lives in us, we rejoice in the Sabbath and rest in the rest of God. We rest from our daily labors so that we can ascend into heaven and worship our Savior, delight in him, enjoy sweet fellowship with the saints, and invite others to enter God's rest.

Question 44

How do we love those who are in a higher or lower position than ourselves?

We love our neighbors who are in a high or
low estate by affording to them either proper
respect and honor or fatherly/motherly care.

The principle of synecdoche helps us to understand God's law and
how to apply his law in our lives. In Deuteronomy 5, we read the
Ten Commandments, but the rest of the book is in many ways an
exposition of them. God's law has manifold applications.

We are to honor our mother and father. But who are they? Is this
simply a commandment for children who have one or two parents?
The vast majority of theologians over the history of the church
have rightly recognized that the Bible uses the terms "mother" and
"father" in various ways: biological, spiritual (e.g., Christ says,
"Who is my mother?" Matt. 12:48), and authoritative (e.g., family,
church, state).

Paul offers us a glimpse into a practical application of the fifth
commandment in his first letter to Timothy:

Do not rebuke an older man but encourage him as you would a father, younger men as brothers, older women as mothers, younger women as sisters, in all purity. Honor widows who are truly widows. But if a widow has children or grandchildren, let them first learn to show godliness to their own household and to make some return to their parents, for this is pleasing in the sight of God. (1 Tim. 5:1–4)

The outworking of love in the church gets highlighted by the peculiar responsibilities we have to others, whether older or younger, male or female. To give is to receive. Thus we treat an older man like a father in order that he, who has a type of authority, may treat the younger with love and tenderness (2 Cor. 12:14–15). When those in authority show love and tenderness, those under their authority will submit more willingly and cheerfully (1 Cor. 4:14–16).

This commandment of love has important ramifications for how we honor our superiors, including those in political authority. For example, applied to Americans, the fifth commandment requires them to honor the president. Even if we disagree with the actions and policies of a specific president (or prime minister or leader of another title), we must, as the Westminster Larger Catechism says, offer

all due reverence in heart, word, and behaviour; prayer and thanksgiving for them; imitation of their virtues and graces; willing obedience to their lawful commands and counsels; due submission to their corrections; fidelity to, defense and maintenance of their persons and authority, according to their several ranks, and the nature of their places; bearing with their infirmities, and covering them in love, that so they may be an honour to them and to their government. (q. 127)

Showing this type of honor is the best way to keep us from sinning against our superiors. We have duties toward them. We cannot rebel against their lawful commands. Moreover, we cannot curse or mock them because God himself institutes them:

> Let every person be subject to the governing authorities. For there is no authority except from God, and those that exist have been instituted by God. Therefore whoever resists the authorities resists what God has appointed, and those who resist will incur judgment. For rulers are not a terror to good conduct, but to bad. Would you have no fear of the one who is in authority? Then do what is good, and you will receive his approval, for he is God's servant for your good. But if you do wrong, be afraid, for he does not bear the sword in vain. For he is the servant of God, an avenger who carries out God's wrath on the wrongdoer. Therefore one must be in subjection, not only to avoid God's wrath but also for the sake of conscience. For because of this you also pay taxes, for the authorities are ministers of God, attending to this very thing. Pay to all what is owed to them: taxes to whom taxes are owed, revenue to whom revenue is owed, respect to whom respect is owed, honor to whom honor is owed. (Rom. 13:1–7)

This passage applies the fifth commandment in terms of how we relate to the state. The apostle Paul uses strong language. Even if we determine that our leader is an "enemy," we are still required to love our enemies. The way we love those in authority, for example, is by praying for them instead of cursing them (Luke 6:27–28). We are to pray for our rulers (1 Tim. 2:2).

Those who are in authority also have important duties toward their subordinates as part of their fatherly care. It is hard to improve on the language of the Westminster Larger Catechism on this point:

Q. 129. What is required of superiors towards their inferiors?

A. It is required of superiors, according to that power they receive from God, and that relation wherein they stand, to love, pray for, and bless their inferiors; to instruct, counsel, and admonish them; countenancing, commending, and rewarding such as do well; and discountenancing, reproving, and chastising such as do ill; protecting, and providing for them all things necessary for soul and body: and by grave, wise, holy, and exemplary carriage, to procure glory to God, honor to themselves, and so to preserve that authority which God hath put upon them.

Importantly, the Westminster divines begin with love ("to love"), and what follows is really an exposition of what love looks like from a "superior" to an "inferior." A member in the church, for example, owes respect and honor to the pastor because of the position the pastor occupies as Christ's earthly representative (Heb. 13:7). But it is not one-way love. The pastor must, among other things, pray for and bless those under his authority.

Nearly all people find themselves in roles of both authority and submission, often simultaneously. Regardless of our role, God demands love to all, whether superiors or subordinates. The fifth commandment provides the basis for why we should love and how we should love those who exercise authority over us and those over whom we exercise authority.

Question 45

What obedience should Christian parents expect from their children?

Children must offer loving obedience
to their parents "in the Lord."

When Paul addresses children in the church, he does so with the type of language that should give us pause. In two places in particular, he addresses them with regard to their obedience to their parents: first, in Ephesians 6:1, Paul commands children to obey "in the Lord"; second, in Colossians 3:20, he informs them that obedience "pleases the Lord."

What does it mean for children to obey "in the Lord"? We can note a number of observations. First, since Paul is using language explicitly taken from the Decalogue in Ephesians 6:1–3, we may say that God's view of children and his expectations of children are no different whether in the old or new covenant. Second, Paul uses the language of union with Christ toward these children as the proper basis for their obedience. This second thought needs more explication.

Obedience manifests love. Children are to love their parents, but they are also to love the Lord by obeying their parents. Since the children are to obey "in the Lord," we may rightly conclude that Paul addresses these children as Christians in the same way he refers to others in the letter. Thus, children are to obey in light of all the realities spoken of in terms of union with Christ in the letter to the Ephesians. God does not require of them true obedience apart from a gracious context of response to his saving purposes. True obedience, in the Lord, always flows out of the indicatives of his grace.

These points also help us to make sense of Paul's language in Colossians 3:20. He addresses the Colossians as "God's chosen ones, holy and beloved" (v. 12). He speaks to them about their conduct toward others and how they are to forgive one another as the Lord has forgiven them (v. 13). "Above all these," says Paul, "put on love, which binds everything together in perfect harmony" (v. 14). Paul then specifically addresses wives and husbands (vv. 18–19) and then children (v. 20). Wives and husbands clearly relate to each other not only in light of the specific commands of verses 18–19 but also in light of the immediate and larger context of Colossians. Is Paul expecting anything different from the children in verse 20?

God is pleased with the obedience of children because they are obeying "in the Lord." Obedience "outside the Lord" cannot please God, for whatever is not of faith is sin (Rom. 14:23). Unbelievers must still obey the commandments, but such can never be described as "in the Lord [Jesus Christ]" for the simple reason that they are not "in Christ."

In light of the fifth commandment, children must learn that they are not God. Indwelling sin in the heart of any person means there is an ongoing battle between that person and God. Such conflict occurs by disregarding and disobeying parents. When children disobey their parents, they reject the God who made them and takes care of them.

Parents should represent God to their children. But parents are not God. Parents are to have the mind of God and Christ toward their children. Instead of a "because I say so" attitude, parents should be constantly asking their children, "What does the Lord require of you in this situation?" We are not God, as if we have absolute authority. We have a delegated authority, whereby we are to train our children in the Lord. We have responsibilities to our children just as they have toward us.

Indeed, to the degree that we understand the responsibilities of "superiors" toward "inferiors" (see the previous chapter), we will have gone a long way toward drawing out of our children the type of obedience that pleases the Lord. We lose our children when the roles are reversed and they become, practically speaking, "superiors," because we become obedient to their every wish and desire.

Since parents and children in Christian households share the same identity, namely, being "in Christ," their repentance toward each other should look the same. Repentance is a saving grace, whereby the sinner in Christ owns sin and seeks forgiveness, knowing that the latter should be available on the horizontal level (i.e., human and human) because it is always available to repentant sinners on the (much more important) vertical level (i.e., human and God).

Obedience may be truly said to be loving obedience when there is a proper context for such obedience. That context is the church, whereby all are to show proper honor, respect, and fatherly/motherly care in the knowledge that we do so in the Lord for his honor and glory.

Finally, reward is promised for obedience in the fifth commandment, both in Ephesians 6:1–3 and in Colossians 3:20–24. To "live long in the land" may be a temporal promise that also points to a future reward of eternal life (Eph. 6:3). In Colossians 3:23–24, Paul concludes his section by informing those he has addressed, including Christian bondservants, that as we obey "for the Lord" we will receive "from the Lord" an inheritance as our reward. The promising God promises rewards for obedience in the fifth commandment.

Question 46

Why are we to have love and respect for human life?

Because humans are made in the image of God.

As an outgrowth of our love for others, God commands us to treat other humans with respect. The basis for this command goes back to creation. In Genesis 1:26–27, we read,

> Then God said, "Let us make man in our image, after our likeness. And let them have dominion over the fish of the sea and over the birds of the heavens and over the livestock and over all the earth and over every creeping thing that creeps on the earth."
>
> So God created man in his own image,
>   in the image of God he created him;
>   male and female he created them.

Human beings are made in God's image, and for that reason, we are to respect human life. Even the entrance of sin into the world has not changed our basic outlook on our duties toward others. James speaks of the violation of the sixth commandment ("You shall not murder," Ex. 20:13) in terms of how we use our tongue toward others: "With it we bless our Lord and Father, and with it we curse people who are made in the likeness of God" (James 3:9). Any unwarranted harm toward another human being is a violation of the sixth commandment, which always has in view the fact that others are made in God's image.

God's attitude toward human life after the flood shows his love and respect for human life. In Genesis 9, through his covenant with Noah, who stands typologically as head of a new humanity in a new creation, God gracioiusly makes three basic provisions regarding human life:

1. The propagation of life: "Be fruitful and multiply" (vv. 1, 7).
2. The sustenance of life: "Every moving thing that lives shall be food for you" (v. 3).
3. The protection of life: "Whoever sheds the blood of man, by man shall his blood be shed, for God made man in his own image" (v. 6).

The principle of "a life for a life" emerges here, which later gets confirmed in Exodus 21:23–24: "But if there is harm, then you shall pay life for life, eye for eye." God values human life because we are made in his image. Murdering another human being wrongly takes the life of a creature that is most like God.

Any unlawful harm to oneself or a human being is a direct attack on God because we are made in his image. This is why abortion is such an evil crime: it is an attack on him first and foremost before it is an attack on the child, mother, father, or society. As the psalmist says, "For you formed my inward parts; you knitted me together in my mother's womb. I praise you, for I am fearfully and wonderfully made" (Ps. 139:13–14). Since God is the author of human life—the creatures who are made in his image—the killing of infants in the womb is an attack on God.

As a result, the greatest crime in history was not Adam's first sin but the killing of the Lord of glory (1 Cor. 2:8). We are made in God's image, but Christ is the "image of God" (2 Cor. 4:4; cf. Col. 1:15). This statement has all sorts of implications for our theology. But at the very least, because the Son of God is the God-man, there is meaning to human life in this world. There is hope for humanity, whereas for animals, flowers, and stars, there is none. Thus, to murder another person made in God's image is especially heinous because Christ's work has given hope to individuals who are commanded everywhere to repent and turn to Christ (Acts 17:30).

Question 47

How are we to show our love and respect for human life?

We show our love and respect for human life by doing everything we can to preserve human life and by refraining from anything that could unlawfully harm it.

We show love by preserving human life, and hatred by harming it. We are seriously misguided if we believe that actual murder (the literal taking of another human life) is the only breach of the sixth commandment. This injunction requires that we show love in a multitude of ways to our neighbors and ourselves. Godefridus Udemans well notes concerning the sixth commandment, "The purpose of this commandment is to protect people against physical injury and violence. That means we must harm neither ourselves nor anyone else out of malice, nor insult them in thought, word, or deeds, but rather protect our neighbors' lives as our own."[1]

There are a whole host of ways in which this commandment applies to us. We keep the mandate to preserve life when we take good and proper medicine for our various maladies (Isa. 38:21).

Or when we sleep and rest: "It is in vain that you rise up early and go late to rest, eating the bread of anxious toil; for he gives to his beloved sleep" (Ps. 127:2). Not getting enough sleep—which differs from person to person, of course—can be a failure to keep the sixth commandment. Recreations are also beneficial, for Paul says, "Bodily training is of some value" (1 Tim. 4:8).

Moreover, we show love through keeping the sixth commandment when we have charitable thoughts toward others (see 1 Sam. 19:4–5) or when we show compassion, as the Good Samaritan did on his journey (Luke 10:33–34). The Good Samaritan kept the sixth commandment by preserving life. Courteous speech is also another way in which we can show love to others. Peter exhorts his hearers to have certain dispositions and attitudes toward each other:

> Finally, all of you, have unity of mind, sympathy, brotherly love, a tender heart, and a humble mind. Do not repay evil for evil or reviling for reviling, but on the contrary, bless, for to this you were called, that you may obtain a blessing. For
>
> "Whoever desires to love life
>   and see good days,
> let him keep his tongue from evil
>   and his lips from speaking deceit;
> let him turn away from evil and do good;
>   let him seek peace and pursue it." (1 Pet. 3:8–11)

Many churches read the Ten Commandments each week, which, while constructive in many ways, can become problematic. Namely, Christians become too accustomed to hearing the "negative" side of the commandment ("do not murder") and thus miss the positive. For example, many fail to understand that 1 Peter 3:8–11 expresses in a detailed way the duty to preserve life based on the sixth commandment. This is the goal of love. As Peter says earlier in his letter, "Having purified your souls by your obedience to the truth for a sincere brotherly love, love one another earnestly from a pure heart" (1 Pet. 1:22).

Love also forbids us from thinking and doing certain things to our neighbors and ourselves. Not only murder but also thoughts or purposes to kill are forbidden. So, for example, the plot to kill Paul, even though it failed, is viewed in Scripture as evil (Acts 23:12, 16–17, 21, 27). If we tempt others into dangerous situations, then we are also not showing love (Prov. 1:10–11, 15–16). We may also use words that unnecessarily provoke when a soft answer would do much good (Prov. 15:1). Even rejoicing over our enemies' misfortune shows hate instead of love (Prov. 24:17–18). Ridiculing and deriding others likewise fails to show love (Prov. 6:12–14; Matt. 27:39).

Hatred and anger are sins that beset many Christians. These sins are the antithesis of love. Our Lord, in the Sermon on the Mount, says,

> You have heard that it was said to those of old, "You shall not murder; and whoever murders will be liable to judgment." But I say to you that everyone who is angry with his brother will be liable to judgment; whoever insults his brother will be liable to the council; and whoever says, "You fool!" will be liable to the hell of fire. (Matt. 5:21–22)

Here we see how the law is spiritual (Rom. 7:14). When we show anger, we murder. Anger is dangerous and destroys a person, both physically and spiritually. For this reason Paul says, "Let all bitterness and wrath and anger and clamor and slander be put away from you, along with all malice. Be kind to one another, tenderhearted, forgiving one another, as God in Christ forgave you" (Eph. 4:31–32). He shows that we must not merely "put away" or "put off" but that we must also replace what we put off, such as malice, with something positive, such as kindness (see also Col. 3:5–10). In Christian conduct, we indeed refrain from doing bad things, but at the heart of such behavior, we replace our sinful acts with righteous ones. It is the "great exchange" in sanctification. We do not merely cease to hate, but we also put on love.

At the root of sinful anger is pride. We believe things should go our way, and when they do not, we readily become angry. Such behavior shows hatred toward God, because we refuse to accept his providential dealings in our lives.

Much of the sixth commandment actually forms the majority of Paul's description of love in 1 Corinthians 13. Notice Paul's language: "Love is patient and kind; love does not envy or boast; it is not arrogant or rude. It does not insist on its own way; it is not irritable or resentful; it does not rejoice at wrongdoing, but rejoices with the truth" (vv. 4–6). Patience and kindness directly fulfill the sixth commandment. Envy, boasting, arrogance, and rudeness, while not limited to this commandment, certainly do violate it. To insist on one's own way or to be irritable or resentful is likewise a failure to properly understand how we can "preserve" human life (i.e., build it up psychologically, emotionally, and spiritually). God forbids wrongdoing to one's neighbor; therefore, we are committed, in love, to right doing in every way possible and lawful. Anger, along with everything attached to this vice, is a wide-ranging sin.

The solutions to anger and hatred are various, but we must first recognize that our anger does not actually help make things better for others or us, "for the anger of man does not produce the righteousness of God" (James 1:20). The solution is to put on love and cultivate charitable thoughts and words toward others. Moreover, we must learn to accept that God is ultimately in control and that our anger with life's situations, at its core, reflects our disapproval of the way God is dealing with us. Jesus is the "center of the world"; we are not.

Question 48

What are our sexual duties in this life, and how does the fulfillment of such manifest love?

These duties include maintaining pure thoughts and actions and sexually satisfying our spouse out of love that prefers the other.

As murder begins with the heart, so too does adultery (Matt. 5:27–28).[1] God's desire for his people involves wholehearted purity in all our thoughts and actions. Paul speaks to the Thessalonians of God's will for us in sanctification: "that you abstain from sexual immorality; that each one of you know how to control his own body in holiness and honor, not in the passion of lust like the Gentiles who do not know God" (1 Thess. 4:3–5).

The Scriptures are full of explicit and implicit warnings about sexual sins. Fundamentally, sexual sin concerns not so much the act as the impurity of our hearts. Therefore, there exists a need for constant purification (2 Cor. 7:1; 1 John 3:3). Without purity in our hearts by faith in the power of the Holy Spirit, our hearts run wild with all manner of unholy sexual thoughts, which very often lead to perverse actions.

This is Paul's point in Romans 1:24–27, where he says that God gives up the ungodly "in the lusts of their hearts to impurity," which leads to "dishonorable passions" whereby women and men engage in unnatural relations with people of the same sex. The heart is where sin begins, but that does not mean our sin ends at the heart.

Like Job, we should be watchful over our eyes: "I have made a covenant with my eyes; how then could I gaze at a virgin?" (Job 31:1). Our "eyes" reflect the state of our heart. To lust after another person shows hate, not love. This is why men must treat the "younger women as sisters, in all purity" (1 Tim. 5:2).

To commit adultery in the heart and in the flesh is self-serving. In no way can adulterous thoughts be conceived as loving. Once we move from the heart to the eyes, actions are never far behind (James 1:13–15) unless mortification takes place (Rom. 8:13).

Those in the flesh have "eyes full of adultery, insatiable for sin" (2 Pet. 2:14); they are given to sin. But even those in the Spirit still sin. Even the most sanctified saint, with blood running through his or her veins, likely has a problem with lust of some form.

Masturbation involves unchecked, unmortified lust. It remains a common sin, especially among young men. It has been said, "Except for holy men, heroes, and hypocrites, everybody has masturbated."[2] Indeed. We could deal with the sin of masturbation by describing the isolationism of a man or woman pleasuring him or herself as utterly ridiculous. A man or woman hidden alone in a bathroom or bedroom masturbating is a tragedy. A married man doing the same thing makes the act even more tragic. Such a pathetic picture, though, will not likely stop a person from self-gratification.

Masturbation naturally and quickly leads to unclean thoughts.

True, such can happen anywhere at any time, but we are deluded if we think we can keep our minds morally neutral while masturbating. In deciding whether masturbation is wrong, we might ask the following questions of all practices where we don't have an explicit text:

1. Am I given to it, or is it given to me? For Christians, the dominion of sin is broken; sin no longer has mastery over us (Romans 6).
2. Does this create an invisible barrier between God and me (i.e., hinder my prayers; cf. 1 Pet. 3:7)?
3. Can I give thanks to God after doing this? We are to give thanks in all circumstances (1 Thess. 5:18).
4. Does this cultivate love for God or my neighbor (1 Cor. 14:1; 16:14)?

The act of masturbation strikes out against the Trinity, which entails a loving communion of persons. True love is always a giving love. The triune God eternally loves with a perfect operation of love between the three persons, where there is infinite giving and receiving.

God thus gives sexual gratification for the mutual pleasure of a man and woman in the estate of marriage (Song of Songs; Heb. 13:4). When one spouse masturbates, he or she chooses the path of self instead of sacrificing for the other (cf. Luke 9:23). On the contrary, husbands and wives are expected to serve each other by satisfying each other sexually. In fact, for married couples, the seventh commandment not only forbids adultery but also commands sexual intimacy between a husband and wife. Paul speaks to the positive side of the seventh commandment in his first letter to the Corinthians:

> The husband should give to his wife her conjugal rights, and likewise the wife to her husband. For the wife does not have

authority over her own body, but the husband does. Likewise the husband does not have authority over his own body, but the wife does. Do not deprive one another, except perhaps by agreement for a limited time, that you may devote yourselves to prayer; but then come together again, so that Satan may not tempt you because of your lack of self-control. (1 Cor. 7:3–5)

Husbands and wives fulfill the seventh commandment when they both aim to satisfy each other sexually (Prov. 5:18–19). A consistent pattern of withholding sexual intimacy from one's spouse is a violation of the seventh commandment. Of course, love also means that husbands and wives must show mutual understanding and sympathy for each other, which may involve a degree of self-denial in certain instances from one spouse in particular (usually the man). For sex to be honorable, it must reflect love. There must be mutual giving and receiving.

Question 49

What is the primary mark of a Christian marriage?

The primary mark of a Christian marriage is love
that reflects the union of Christ and the church.

The love that a Christian man and a Christian woman show to each other in marriage has a peculiar dignity that is not shared by all marriages. Love in a Christian marriage is a beautiful picture of the gospel: a picture of Christ and the church.

Many suppose that the man's duty in marriage is to love his wife, whereas the wife's duty is to submit to her husband. This is true, but the wife has the same fundamental duty—to love: "Older women . . . are to teach what is good, and so train the young women to love their husbands" (Titus 2:3–4).

Love issues forth different expectations of husbands and wives. God most importantly demands of those in marriage that they glorify him by accepting that he knows what is best for husbands and wives. By first acknowledging his right to offer us specific commands in marriage, we can then love our spouse first for the Lord's sake and second for his or her sake.

The seventh commandment finds its clearest expression in light of the grand gospel truths concerning Christ's voluntary, sacrificial death on behalf of his bride. Leading up to that truth, Paul commands wives to submit to their husbands, but it is submission "as to the Lord" (Eph. 5:22). Submission is highlighted in other places: "Wives, submit to your husbands, as is fitting in the Lord" (Col. 3:18; see also 1 Pet. 3:1–7). A wife's submission to her husband is an expression of her loving trust toward the Lord and of her love for her husband. As the church submits in everything to Christ out of love, so wives submit in everything out of love (Eph. 5:24). Respect toward husbands remains one way that love comes to expression in a marriage (Eph. 5:33).

Husbands are commanded to love their wives (Eph. 5:25), but their love is not without definition. It must look a certain way. In fact, it is a demanding love because husbands must love their wives as Christ loved the church (Eph. 5:25). All love is sacrificial, but the husband leads in this respect by sacrificing for his wife as he seeks to honor the Lord and do good to his wife. Not only sacrifice but also "cherish[ing]" is an aspect of a husband's love for his wife (Eph. 5:28–29). A husband unwilling to lay down his life for his wife is not worthy to be a husband. St. John Chrysostom's words are deeply moving in terms of what young husbands ought to say to their wives:

> I have taken you in my arms, and I love you, and I prefer you to my life itself. For the present life is nothing, and my most ardent dream is to spend it with you in such a way that we may be assured of not being separated in the life reserved for us. . . . I place your love above all things, and nothing would be more bitter or painful to me than to be of a different mind than you.[1]

That is what it means to keep the seventh commandment—and to do so with some degree of joy. Moreover, for those who have children, one of the greatest gifts a husband and wife can give to their children is not gold or silver but an example of a loving relationship that mirrors Christ and the church. We love our children when we as spouses love each other in the way God has commanded. Any form of hatred toward our spouse is not only hatred toward our spouse and God but also toward our children.

Question 50

Why is adultery such a heinous sin?

Adultery is so heinous because it betrays the faithful love of the Lord Jesus Christ, violates the marriage covenant, destroys the lives of innocent people, and involves several other sins against God and man.

As image bearers of God, and specifically of Christ, we take his name in vain when we engage in sinful lusts and practices. As we live holy lives acceptable and pleasing to God, we hallow his name (John 15:8). In keeping the third commandment, we bring glory to Christ, who himself is glorified in us (John 17:10).

When we sin, especially in publicly grievous ways, we profane the name of God and Christ. The point is that we as Christians wear the name of Jesus Christ before an unbelieving world. Baptism is a tattoo, a "tribal marker," so to speak. When we commit adultery, we tear that name from our shoulder and trample on the blood of the covenant (see Ex. 28:12, 29–30).

Adultery is more grievous than fornication because when adultery takes place, we break the conjugal bond between a man and woman who made vows to each other. Not all fornication involves adultery, but all adultery involves fornication.

Adultery profanes God's name, especially in a Christian marriage. The adulterer places his will over and against God's. Therefore, adultery is a form of idolatry. Paul highlights the heinousness of adultery and sexual immorality when he argues that the sexually immoral person "sins against his own body," whereas other sins are committed outside the body (1 Cor. 6:18). Since our bodies are temples of the Holy Spirit (1 Cor. 6:19), we are not our own. Christ died for us—we were bought with a price—and so we must glorify God in our bodies. Adultery goes against Christ's glory.

Since sexual union for a married couple is the becoming of "one flesh" (1 Cor. 6:16), adultery severs that one-flesh union. The most intimate union between two humans is the sexual union between husband and wife. Adultery breaks that fleshly bond. Thus, adultery remains one of the few legitimate grounds for divorce. In the Old Testament, adultery was punishable by death (Lev. 20:10; Num. 5:11–31; Deut. 22:22–24). In Matthew 19:4–9, our Lord explains that divorce is permissible but not necessary when adultery takes place. Not every sin provides allowable grounds for divorce, but adultery does.

Adultery shows hatred against our neighbor. It also violates the eighth commandment ("You shall not steal," Ex. 20:15). As Thomas Watson notes, "It is the highest sort of theft. The adulterer steals from his neighbor that which is more than his goods and estate; he steals away his wife from him, who is flesh of his flesh."[1] The adulterer also covets someone not rightly his or hers.

Furthermore, adultery involves self-hatred because it cannot possibly do anything good for the one committing it:

> He who commits adultery lacks sense;
>   he who does it destroys himself.

He will get wounds and dishonor,
   and his disgrace will not be wiped away. (Prov. 6:32–33)

Watson again makes a salient point:

> Some, when they get wounds, get honor. The soldiers' wounds are full of honor; the martyr's wounds for Christ are full of honor; but the adulterer gets wounds, but no honor to his name. . . . Wounds of reputation no physician can heal. When the adulterer dies, his shame lives.[2]

We are to love ourselves appropriately, but adultery is just about the last way we can show love to ourselves.

Ultimately, adultery, because it is a willful sin, reveals that we are not content with the love Christ has for us or with his provisions for us in marriage. What the Roman soldiers did to Christ on the cross by driving a spear into his side is not much different from the adulterer who rams his spear into the side of the person's spouse he or she is taking.

Question 51

How does love manifest itself in regard to our worldly goods and name?

Love manifests itself in regard to our worldly goods and name when expressed in a spirit of trust toward God and generosity toward man.

In the garden of Eden, Adam broke the eighth commandment when he allowed Eve to take from the tree what God commanded them not to eat (Gen. 3:17). They stole. But their theft was a result of distrust toward God. At the heart of stealing is a spirit of distrust.

Like every sin, theft occurs first against God and only second against man. Judas, for example, lacked love toward God and his neighbor. Hence, John writes, "[Judas] said this, not because he cared about the poor, but because he was a thief, and having charge of the moneybag he used to help himself to what was put into it" (John 12:6). If Judas actually loved the poor, he would not have stolen from them. And more fundamentally, if Judas trusted in Christ's gracious provisions for him, he would not have stolen.

Many people, including Christians, break the eighth commandment. Students cheat on tests, adults are dishonest on their taxes, and many steal music online without paying. Less obvious but no less wicked are the sins of envy and idleness. Paul even speaks to the Thessalonians about idleness: "For we hear that some among you walk in idleness, not busy at work, but busybodies" (2 Thess. 3:11). Failing to care for one's family is also theft (1 Tim. 5:8).

So many rob their employers through "theft of time," which is likely the most common form of theft that goes unpunished today. Many start late, finish early, stretch their break time, and work less than 100 percent. That is theft. Unlawful callings, whereby a job causes you to sin (e.g., prostitution, casino work, fortune telling), is also theft because it causes others to sin (see Acts 19:18–19, 24–25). Bribery too is theft (Prov. 15:27). Slander is a particularly heinous form of stealing. Iago's words in Shakespeare's *Othello* are haunting in this respect:

> A good reputation is the most valuable thing we have—men and women alike. If you steal my money, you're just stealing trash. It's something, it's nothing: it's yours, it's mine, and it'll belong to thousands more. But if you steal my reputation, you're robbing me of something that doesn't make you richer, but makes me much poorer.[1]

In all these sins, a failure to trust God and be generous toward our neighbor manifests itself. Selfishness, unbelief, and pride are all present when we violate the eighth commandment. Love is missing because love trusts God for who he is and goes the extra mile with our neighbor.

The Scriptures are not silent on what it means to keep the eighth commandment. Consider the example of Zacchaeus, the chief tax collector, for whom conversion meant that a thief became generous:

And Zacchaeus stood and said to the Lord, "Behold, Lord, the half of my goods I give to the poor. And if I have defrauded anyone of anything, I restore it fourfold." And Jesus said to him, "Today salvation has come to this house, since he also is a son of Abraham. For the Son of Man came to seek and to save the lost." (Luke 19:8–10)

Zacchaeus put into practice what Paul commends to the Ephesians: "Let the thief no longer steal, but rather let him labor, doing honest work with his own hands, so that he may have something to share with anyone in need" (Eph. 4:28). This statement applies the eighth commandment positively. The spirit of generosity flows out of the Spirit-filled life. Christians, so far as they have the ability and opportunity, are to "do good to everyone, and especially to those who are of the household of faith" (Gal. 6:10).

In the Westminster Larger Catechism, the divines ask, "What are the duties required in the eighth commandment?" (q. 141). In part the answer reads, "Endeavor, by all just and lawful means, to procure, preserve, and further the wealth and outward estate of others, as well as our own" (Gen. 47:14; Matt. 22:39; Phil. 2:4). In other words, when Paul says, "Let each of you look not only to his own interests, but also to the interests of others" (Phil. 2:4), he is applying the eighth commandment. We thus look to God's interests by honoring him appropriately, especially as we trust him to provide for us in this life. We also look to our neighbors' interests by furthering their wealth—a most remarkable statement—as an act of love toward them. But we are also commanded to keep this commandment by furthering our own estate, so long as we do so lawfully.

Much is at stake here. We are trustees of everything we own, just as we are trustees of the talents God has given us. Unless we live with a constant eye on trusting a good God who provides and on attending to our neighbor, for whom we must also try to provide, we will end up with the spirit of Judas, who only outwardly made great claims about his care for the poor but in reality was a self-serving unbeliever.

Question 52

How is our generosity in love to be shown in the local church?

Generosity is shown in the local church by
giving ourselves first to kingdom work.

In the Presbyterian Church in America (PCA), new members make vows by responding affirmatively to five different questions. In one of those questions, new members are asked, "Do you promise to support the Church in its worship and work to the best of your ability?"[1] This is an exceedingly important question because Christians are to love the church. They are to seek first the kingdom of God (Matt. 6:33). As those who were once former members of Satan's kingdom (2 Cor. 4:4; Eph. 2:1–2), we have switched allegiances (Col. 1:13–14). Daily we pray, "Your kingdom come" (Matt. 6:10).

Kingdom life demands total commitment. We pluck out eyes in this kingdom and cut off offending hands (Matt. 5:29–30). In fact, we must be willing to hate, if required, our father, mother, brother, and sister—even our own lives—for the sake of the kingdom (Luke 14:26). That is what it means for the kingdom to come first.

God has given us various gifts to be used in the church for the building of his kingdom on earth. For example, God brings wealthy people to faith not only for his own glory but also for the sake of the kingdom. Consider Paul's exhortation:

> As for the rich in this present age, charge them not to be haughty, nor to set their hopes on the uncertainty of riches, but on God, who richly provides us with everything to enjoy. They are to do good, to be rich in good works, to be generous and ready to share, thus storing up treasure for themselves as a good foundation for the future, so that they may take hold of that which is truly life. (1 Tim. 6:17–19)

By giving to the kingdom, we can never lose. God promises a reward to giving done in faith. How we handle money very often reveals our spiritual condition. After all, "no one can serve two masters, for either he will hate the one and love the other, or he will be devoted to the one and despise the other. You cannot serve God and money" (Matt. 6:24). Those who leave everything to follow Christ are promised a "hundredfold" return and a guarantee that they "will inherit eternal life" (Matt. 19:29).

In 2 Corinthians 8–9, we have a vibrant testimony to the generosity of God as the basis for our own generosity in the kingdom. When Paul addresses the Corinthians, he explains to them very clearly that those who sow sparingly will reap sparingly, whereas those who sow bountifully will reap bountifully (2 Cor. 9:6; see also Gal. 6:6–10). A few observations flow out of 2 Corinthians 9:6:

1. The money we give to kingdom work is not money wasted. Rather, it is seed sown for the kingdom's sake and our sake.
2. When prayerfully considering how much we should give, we should also consider, like a farmer, what kind of harvest we want to reap.

3. Since God makes an explicit promise, we may desire a large reward as a motive to giving.

In the next verse (2 Cor. 9:7), we come to some more observations regarding kingdom giving: "Each one must give as he has decided in his heart, not reluctantly or under compulsion, for God loves a cheerful giver":

1. "Each one": Grace-produced giving is an individual responsibility, which includes children, if they are able, who should be taught to give from a young age.
2. "Decided" equals "purposed": We do so with a purpose, namely, the kingdom.
3. "Not reluctantly": We are to give not grudgingly but as someone with a generous spirit because we serve a faithful, generous God.
4. "Cheerful giver": Paul calls for exhilarated givers—those who might even put a smiley face on the check!
5. "God loves": God sees his Son in us and loves us; he loves us especially when we are most like his Son, who for the joy set before him gave himself for our sins (Heb. 12:2).

There are indeed other ways we seek the kingdom first. Very often it involves not our money but our time and energy. Our generosity as Christians permeates our whole life, not just our checkbook. For some, "cutting a check" is easy, but taking time to pray for the kingdom or taking time to help the needy is a generosity that is far too foreign.

Helping single mothers or aiding seminary students or supporting pastors in third-world countries are just a few of the ways in which we can show our concern to be generous with our whole heart, soul, mind, and strength in the context of kingdom living. Whatever our particular gifting, we have no choice but to be generous in the church. This is how we show our love for one another.

Question 53

Why is lying so serious?

Lying is so serious because love rejoices
with the truth, while lying shows hatred.

Lying is perhaps the most common of sins. The ninth commandment ("You shall not bear false witness against your neighbor," Ex. 20:16) deals with the sin of deception. As Thomas Watson says, "God has set two natural fences to keep in the tongue, the teeth and lips; and this commandment is a third fence set about it, that it should not break forth into evil."[1]

Lying is not a small sin compared to, say, murder. In Revelation 21:8, we are told, "As for the cowardly, the faithless, the detestable, as for murderers, the sexually immoral, sorcerers, idolaters, and all liars, their portion will be in the lake that burns with fire and sulfur, which is the second death."

Satan began his hatred toward mankind by lying; he is thus called "the father of lies" (John 8:44). By nature, all men are liars and deceivers (Rom. 3:13). Cain lied when, after God asked him, "Where is Abel your brother?" he said, "I do not know; am I my brother's keeper?" (Gen. 4:9). Abraham lied and did not trust God on two occasions (Gen. 12:13; 20:2). Laban lied to Jacob, a deceiver in his own right, by not conveying his hidden agenda (Gen. 29:16–30)—a case of the trickster tricked, the deceiver deceived.

Lying involves either an action or inaction, which may be verbal or nonverbal, with an intention to deceive someone for the advantage of the perpetrator. There are various lies, such as malicious lies that are planned and executed. A white lie ("small lie") may still be a malicious lie. There is also what may be termed a jocular lie, when some degree of truth is spoken in jest. Elements of truth cannot always be distinguished, especially when the person has to say, "I was only joking" (cf. Prov. 26:18–19).

At its base, lying reveals a lack of love. In contrast, love "believes all things" and "hopes all things" (1 Cor. 13:7). So when we speak to someone who loves us, we must be careful to speak the truth, for love "rejoices with the truth" (1 Cor. 13:6).

Lying may be allowed only when we show love to our neighbor, that is, we lie for our neighbor's benefit specifically by countering wickedness in dire circumstances. Love dictates the lawfulness of an action. Those who hid Jewish people during the Second World War were lying, but they were not sinfully lying, because their action proceeded from love in the face of death.

When the Hebrew midwives lied to Pharaoh, they acted righteously because they were preserving life by lying (Ex. 1:15–21). They loved others. When Rahab lied to the wicked to save the lives of the spies, she faithfully wore the Lord's name: "By faith Rahab the prostitute did not perish with those who were disobedient, because she had given a friendly welcome to the spies" (Heb. 11:31). In Rahab we have a beautiful picture of faith, hope, and love: love for the Hebrew spies borne from faith that it was the right thing to do, all of which led to hope that her family would not perish (Josh. 2:12–14; see also 1 Sam. 16:2; 2 Sam. 17:20; James 2:25).

Allegedly, Athanasius, when undergoing persecution at the risk of his life, was asked by his pursuers, "Where is Athanasius?" He replied, "Athanasius is not far away; with a little effort you can find him." Here he deceived, but he preserved his life. He was in dire, not difficult, circumstances. These various examples all constitute dire circumstances. Faith and love enable us to use wisdom in this respect if we are ever called to lie righteously. But for the vast majority of the time, lying is wrong because it is usually self-serving and therefore lacks the principle of love.

Why do we lie? We want people to think better of us. That is, we are discontent with the love of God and Christ. We want the admiration of man. If we grasp the love offered to us in the gospel, we know that the eternal God thinks well of us and that we do not need to go looking for scraps among humans.

Fantasy living, which is based not on reality but rather on our mere mental wishes, also explains why we lie. The world of fantasy presents itself as more interesting and appealing to us than the real world. Our lives are boring to us because we have not taken seriously the hope that God has revealed in his Word. Thus, lying is a denial of Christian hope. If we have true hope, we have all the "fantasy" that we could ever need. But discontent with the promises of what God has in store for us, we lie. We are saying, "I do not love God's promises enough to believe them. I do not love God's providential care of my life enough to be content. Therefore, I will lie to make up what God has left out." This is why lying has devastating consequences.

Lying is ultimately against the gospel: it is self-serving instead of self-giving. Falsehood is a reflection more of Satan than of Christ. We must reflect our new husband, not our old father.

Question 54

How do we show love with regard to our speech?

We show love with regard to our speech when we
speak the truth seasonably and in love at all times.

The God of truth, who loves us, shows his love to us by speaking the truth to us. As sinners, we do not naturally welcome truth (John 8:45). We need the Spirit of truth in us to receive divine truth. Even for Christians, receiving the truth can hurt because of the indwelling sin in us that hates the truth. Paul even has to ask the Galatians, whom he loves, "Have I then become your enemy by telling you the truth?" (Gal. 4:16).

God loves truth tellers and invites them to worship him on his holy hill ("he who . . . speaks truth in his heart," Ps. 15:1–2). After all, worship is the ultimate act of truth telling since in worship we speak glorious things of God!

To speak the truth in love is to speak the truth in a certain manner. Paul exhorts the Colossians, "Let your speech always be gracious, seasoned with salt, so that you may know how you ought to answer each person" (Col. 4:6). Speaking the truth in love (Eph. 4:15) is speaking the truth graciously. Gracious speech is always truthful, but true speech may not always be gracious. They key is to bring together truth and grace (love). The restrained use of words with a "cool spirit" is also a way to speak the truth in love (Prov. 17:27). We must speak the truth seasonably (Prov. 29:11).

There may be occasions when silence is better than speaking something that is factually true. Someone may have lost a loved one, and we could say something that would be factually true but still spoken unseasonably. Nonetheless, there are times when true friendship demands a rebuke. As Proverbs 27:6 says, "Faithful are the wounds of a friend; profuse are the kisses of an enemy." Sometimes, out of love, we must address sin in an individual. Christ showed his love to the seven churches by speaking the truth, sometimes painful truth, to them:

> I know your works: you are neither cold nor hot. Would that you were either cold or hot! So, because you are lukewarm, and neither hot nor cold, I will spit you out of my mouth. For you say, I am rich, I have prospered, and I need nothing, not realizing that you are wretched, pitiable, poor, blind, and naked. (Rev. 3:15–17)

John the Baptist spoke truthfully to Herod when he said, "It is not lawful for you to have your brother's wife" (Mark 6:18). He ended up losing his life because he spoke the truth. In contrast, many preachers today are guilty of not speaking the whole truth to their flock. If a preacher is not concerned out of love for people's souls, then he will be concerned out of self-love for personal gain (Ezek. 13:19; Mic. 3:5).

The false prophet desires acceptance: "If a man should go about and utter wind and lies, saying, 'I will preach to you of wine and strong drink,' he would be the preacher for this people!"

(Mic. 2:11). But the true prophet (or pastor) exposes the sin of his people (Ezek. 3:16–21; cf. Lam. 2:14). This is not easy. Hence, Jeremiah had trembling bones and a broken heart (Jer. 23:9). Amos was told to shut up and go home (Amos 7:12–13). And our Lord was murdered for speaking the truth.

This is why, instead of speaking the truth to people, we prefer to flatter. We flatter because we want people to think better of us. As Udemans says, flattery is "speaking so sweetly of others that it is out of proportion to what they really are."[1] Udemans quotes an anonymous Athenian philosopher who compares flatterers with vultures: "Flatterers were worse than vultures, for vultures eat only dead people, while flatterers eat them alive."[2] Flattery is so dangerous because it dresses itself up in love but is really a sophisticated form of hatred.

This means that while love "rejoices with the truth" (1 Cor. 13:6), it can have very painful consequences, even if we speak graciously and seasonably. Do we love people enough to speak to them the truth that may save them, or do we love our self-preservation so much that we will speak to them falsehood or flattery that may damn them?

Love also demands, according to the Westminster Larger Catechism (q. 144), that we readily receive good reports of others, that we discourage tale bearers and slanderers, and that we defend our name and the names of others when needed (especially for the sake of the gospel). What a lovely commandment that seeks the good name of others and does good to others by speaking to them the truth.

Question 55

What keeps us from an inordinate desire for the things of the world?

We avoid an inordinate desire for the things
of the world through our love for our heavenly
Father and our knowledge that he knows what
we need and gives good gifts to his children.

God gives his children many temporal gifts in this world that go
beyond pure need. As a generous God, he does not simply give
to his children the "bare necessities." These gifts are graciously
bestowed on us since we have forfeited our right to anything good
by virtue of our sinfulness. But as humans we have real needs, and
we may desire to be blessed by God with material things because
he is a merciful God.

The Christian life is a life on a knife-edge, so to speak. Many
have seen the rampant greed in this world and decided to pursue
a life of rigorous asceticism. But pursuing an ascetic lifestyle does
nothing to restrain the flesh, because at its core, sinful desire is a
matter of the heart. Thus the commandment "You shall not covet"

brings us back, in many respects, to the first commandment: to have no other gods before the Lord our God.

Covetousness usually begins when we are caught off guard by a desire. The sin emerges not so much in the initial, bare desire as in our response of nursing that particular desire. After feeding and nurturing the desire, we develop a plan for bringing our desire to fruition. The desire and plan then turn into action, and we get (or snatch) something that may not be rightfully ours.

Whether we're considering Achan (Joshua 7) or Ahab and Jezebel (1 Kings 21) or Ananias and Sapphira (Acts 5), we see that covetousness is not a sin God takes lightly. It was the sin that "awoke" the apostle Paul to his own sinfulness (Rom. 7:7–12).

The sin of covetousness is no respecter of persons. We are all surrounded by mass marketing on unprecedented levels. We perhaps do not even realize the degree to which the world is telling us that we need this or that and that we do not have enough and need more. Children do not need to learn to covet. They read pamphlets and see signs, and they naturally want, want, want.

Sin is greedy; it is parasitic. In one of Aesop's fables, we read of the envious man. Zeus would grant him any wish he wanted on the condition that his neighbor would get twice as much. The man wished for the loss of one eye. This is not a stretch of reality by any means.[1]

If we do not deal with our covetous heart, then we are in danger of hell. Paul, writing to the Ephesian Christians, makes this point: "For you may be sure of this, that everyone who is sexually immoral or impure, or who is covetous (that is, an idolater), has no inheritance in the kingdom of Christ and God" (Eph. 5:5).

There are a number of solutions to the problem of covetousness. If we live according to the flesh and let covetousness reign, then we will die. "But," says Paul, "if by the Spirit you put to death the deeds of the body, you will live" (Rom. 8:13). Covetousness must be dealt with "violently."

Besides prayer and the other appointed means of grace (e.g., public worship), we must keep in mind that our God gives good gifts to his children: "What do you have that you did not receive?" (1 Cor. 4:7). Elsewhere, James says, "Every good gift and every perfect gift is from above, coming down from the Father of lights" (James 1:17). For example, when we read, "You shall not covet your neighbor's wife" (Ex. 20:17), those of us who are married have to remember that our gracious God has given us a spouse, and to desire someone else is to be thankless to God for his gracious provision.

A proper view of God and his grace helps us immensely in our fight against our inordinate desire for "things." The author to the Hebrews commands his hearers, "Keep your life free from love of money, and be content with what you have, for he has said, 'I will never leave you nor forsake you.' So we can confidently say, 'The Lord is my helper; I will not fear; what can man do to me?'" (Heb. 13:5). Recognizing that God will not forsake us but will instead take care of us is one way to deal with our sin of covetousness.

Moreover, we must learn to love the right things in life. If we love God and Christ by the Spirit, we will quickly learn that nothing else can make us content in this world if those things do not have the triune God's stamp of approval on them. Our hope in the world to come with all the blessings promised to us in that world should also keep us from the love of money. Singing or reading or meditating on Psalm 16 regularly is a good way to draw our minds to heavenly promises rather than worldly curses.

Faith also believes that God will provide for our needs. Thus, we can be content, which is a great remedy against covetousness. Paul went from being a covetous, unregenerate sinner (Rom. 7:8) to addressing the Ephesian elders with these words: "I coveted no one's silver or gold or apparel. You yourselves know that these hands ministered to my necessities and to those who were with me"

(Acts 20:33–34). By the grace of God, Paul learned to be content whatever the circumstances because he could do all things through Christ who strengthened him (Phil. 4:11, 13).

Covetousness must therefore be replaced with a trust in our heavenly Father for his good provisions for us. He may bless us abundantly with fine cheese and wine, or we may have to settle for crumbs. But in all these circumstances, we will not snatch at what is not rightfully ours for the very simple reason that we do not need to in light of who our Father is.

Question 56

Is love optional for Christians?

No, love is not optional for Christians, for unless
their love exceeds that of the scribes and Pharisees,
they cannot enter the kingdom of heaven.

In the Sermon on the Mount, the Lord speaks of the necessity of his
disciples' righteousness exceeding that of the scribes and Pharisees:
"For I tell you, unless your righteousness exceeds that of the scribes
and Pharisees, you will never enter the kingdom of heaven" (Matt.
5:20). Many people who are familiar with the doctrine of Christ's
imputed righteousness immediately assume that Christ must be
speaking here of imputed righteousness, not imparted righteousness. "For," they ask, "how can one possibly be more righteous
than a Pharisee?"

A cursory glance at the Scriptures, especially our Lord's description of the Pharisees in the Gospel accounts, should give us pause
before we assume too quickly that imputed righteousness is what
is required to "surpass" the scribes and Pharisees. The question
we need to ask ourselves is whether the New Testament actually
portrays the Pharisees as being righteous, loving people.

A strongly polemical tone from the lips of Christ is immediately obvious in the Synoptic Gospels toward the Pharisees. In Matthew's Gospel, we note that the words "hypocrite" and "Pharisee" are virtually synonymous. The scribes, who are mentioned with the Pharisees in Matthew 5:20, are also on the receiving end of Christ's scathing polemic in Matthew 23:1–36. It seems that they are notorious for commanding others to keep laws they themselves refuse to keep. Like the Pharisees, the scribes are hypocrites. In fact, far from keeping God's law, they tithe herbs, which is not required by written law, while they neglect the "weightier matters" of the law (Matt. 23:23).

The story of Simon the Pharisee is one of the most shocking in the New Testament (see Luke 7:36–50). This Pharisee denies basic hospitality to Christ, and one detects in Christ's response to him a degree of pain and sadness. The woman in that account offers a strikingly loving contrast to Simon.

According to the Scriptures, the Pharisees do not actually keep God's law; they "leave the commandment of God and hold to the tradition of men" (Mark 7:8). Legalism is just that: replacing God's laws with man's laws.

The type of righteousness that Christ expects from his disciples is manifestly not in any way the type of righteousness that was performed by the scribes and Pharisees. These religious leaders "clean the outside of the cup and the plate, but inside they are full of greed and self-indulgence" (Matt. 23:25).

To add to this, Christ calls on his hearers to "beware of the scribes . . . who devour widows' houses and for a pretense make long prayers. They will receive the greater condemnation" (Mark 12:38–40). We are also told that the Pharisees were "lovers of money" (Luke 16:14). Their "righteousness" needs to be exceeded, not admired. They were not holy men but godless antinomians and legalists who were ultimately responsible for the greatest crime on earth: killing the Lord of glory.

In the Sermon on the Mount, it is clear that Christ is concerned about the heart. Christianity is, of course, a heart religion—a religion of love. As the apostle Paul says in his letter to Timothy, "The aim of our charge is love that issues from a pure heart and a good conscience and a sincere faith" (1 Tim. 1:5). The pure in heart are blessed, for they—and they alone—shall see God (Matt. 5:8). True worship requires that we do so with a pure heart (Ps. 24:4). And we should desire from God a pure heart (Ps. 51:10).

So what type of people exceed the righteousness of the scribes and Pharisees? Luke describes Zechariah and Elizabeth in the following way: "They were both righteous before God, walking blamelessly in all the commandments and statutes of the Lord" (Luke 1:6). Far from being hypocrites, who only kept the law outwardly as a pretense, Zechariah and Elizabeth, living at the dawn of the new covenant, were faithful Israelites. We must aim to be more like Zechariah and Elizabeth than the scribes and Pharisees.

Christians are "slaves of righteousness" (Rom. 6:18). We hunger and thirst after righteousness (Matt. 5:6) as we are progressively sanctified and made into the image of Christ (Rom. 8:29). These are references not to imputed righteousness but to the righteousness (i.e., habitual holiness) that we must possess if we are to enter heaven. As noted already, we have the right to heaven based on the merit of Christ alone. Only his perfect righteousness, imputed to us through faith, can give us a right to heavenly life. But the path on which we walk to heaven is the "path of righteousness" (i.e., holy living). Our imperfect obedience is still obedience from the heart, unlike that of the scribes and Pharisees. This is the obedience that God is pleased to accept (and reward), because it proceeds from the heart.

Paul writes to the Philippians, "Do all things without grumbling or disputing, that you may be blameless and innocent, children of God without blemish in the midst of a crooked and twisted generation, among whom you shine as lights in the world" (Phil. 2:14–15). Similarly, Romans 8:4 describes believers whose righteousness surpasses the scribes and Pharisees (cf. Ps. 106:3), and the reason is that their obedience is wrought by the Spirit and is thus far more precise and extensive.

Ultimately, that is why Christ can make this demand of us in Matthew 5:20: he knows that he will give what he demands (see Eph. 2:8).

As Christians who have been justified by faith alone and therefore accepted in Christ, we are required to live godly lives. Good works are the way we walk to eternal life (heaven). Christ did not die to make us hypocrites. He died for hypocrites to make us righteous: "He himself bore our sins in his body on the tree, that we might die to sin and live to righteousness" (1 Pet. 2:24). Again, to "live to righteousness" in this context is part of the path of sanctification and inward heart renewal by the power of the Spirit.

This gets to the heart of Paul's concern in 1 Corinthians 13:1–3, where he says,

> If I speak in the tongues of men and of angels, but have not love, I am a noisy gong or a clanging cymbal. And if I have prophetic powers, and understand all mysteries and all knowledge, and if I have all faith, so as to remove mountains, but have not love, I am nothing. If I give away all I have, and if I deliver up my body to be burned, but have not love, I gain nothing.

The Pharisees loved to be seen to be doing things, but they did not love the God for whom they were allegedly doing those things. They lacked love, and because they lacked love, they lacked a righteousness that was acceptable to God. It was not from a heart of flesh but from a heart of stone. We exceed the righteousness of the scribes and Pharisees when we love, however imperfectly, from the heart.

Of faith, hope, and love,
which is the greatest?

Love is the greatest, because it alone will remain in
eternity and because it makes us most like God.

"So now faith, hope, and love abide, these three; but the greatest of
these is love" (1 Cor. 13:13). Paul ends his most excellent description of love by saying that of all the three "divine sisters" (faith,
hope, and love), love is the greatest.

Lombard, quoting Gregory, makes an important point with
regard to faith, hope, and love in this life:

> For as long as we are in this life, we find that in us faith, hope,
> charity, and work are equal to each other because we love as
> much as we believe, and insofar as we love we are certain of
> our hope. For each of the faithful believes as much as he hopes
> and loves, and works as much as he believes, loves, and hopes.[1]

At the same time, Thomas Adams speaks beautifully to the truth
that love is the greatest:

[Love] excels in beauty. We may say of this sister, as it was said of the good woman, "Many daughters have done virtuously, but thou excellest them all," Proverbs 31:29. Paul does not disparage any when he says, [Love] is the greatest, 1 Corinthians 13:13. All stars are bright, though one star may differ from another in glory. We may say of graces, as of the captains of the sons of Gad; "the least a hundred, the greatest a thousand." Or as the song was of Saul and David: "Saul hath slain his thousands, David his ten thousands." Faith is excellent, so is Hope; but "the greatest of these is [Love]."[2]

To be a Christian, one must possess faith, hope, and love. To miss one is to miss them all; to have one is to have them all. They all depend on one another. We believe in God's love; we hope for God's love; and we love him for his love. Yet love is the greatest because its limits extend beyond the limits of faith and hope. We believe for ourselves in order to be justified. We hope for ourselves in order to receive what is promised. But we love not only for ourselves but also for others.

The limits of love extend into eternity. Faith receives the whole Christ, so that we are, at the moment of believing, in possession of all that we will ever inherit. Hope expects the promises to be fulfilled and waits in eager expectation. But faith and hope will have an end when we no longer walk by faith but arrive to our destiny of sight. Then all we will need is love.

Faith and hope can give us nothing in heaven that love cannot give us better. In glory, we shall eternally love the Father, Son, and Holy Spirit. We shall love them for their distinct works toward us and in us. We shall love them for what they will continually reveal to us. In heaven, we shall also love our brothers and sisters in the Lord. Heaven is a world of love where righteousness dwells.

In a sermon on 1 Corinthians 13:8–10, Jonathan Edwards

highlights in detail how heaven is a world of love by reflecting on 1 John 4:8:

> The Apostle tells us that God is love, 1 John 4:8. And therefore seeing he is an infinite Being, it follows that he is an infinite fountain of love. Seeing he is an all-sufficient Being, it follows that he is a full and overflowing and an inexhaustible fountain of love. Seeing he is an unchangeable and eternal Being, he is an unchangeable and eternal source of love. There even in heaven dwells that God from whom every stream of holy love, yea, every drop that is or ever was proceeds.
>
> There dwells God the Father, and so the Son, who are united in infinitely dear and incomprehensible mutual love. There dwells God the Father, who is the Father of mercies, and so the Father of love, who so loved the world that he gave his only begotten Son, that whosoever believeth in him should not perish, but have everlasting life [John 3:16]. There dwells Jesus Christ, the Lamb of God, the Prince of peace and love, who so loved the world that he shed his blood, and poured out his soul unto death for it. There dwells the Mediator, by whom all God's love is expressed to the saints, by whom the fruits of it have been purchased, and through whom they are communicated, and through whom love is imparted to the hearts of all the church. There Christ dwells in both his natures, his human and divine, sitting with the Father in the same throne. There is the Holy Spirit, the spirit of divine love, in whom the very essence of God, as it were, all flows out or is shed abroad in the hearts of all the church [cf. Rom. 5:5]. There in heaven this fountain of love, this eternal three in one, is set open without any obstacle to hinder access to it. There this glorious God is manifested and shines forth in full glory, in beams of love; there the fountain overflows in streams and rivers of love and delight, enough for all to drink at, and to swim in, yea, so as to overflow the world as it were with a deluge of love.[3]

Love is the greatest of faith, hope, and love because heaven will be a "deluge of love," not a deluge of hope or faith.

At bottom, faith and hope do not make us like God, but love does. God himself does not believe, and he does not hope. But God loves, for he is love (1 John 4:8). Faith and hope are received from God, but love gives back to God. We shall forever be returning our affections to God through love.

"So now faith, hope, and love abide, these three; but the greatest of these is love" (1 Cor. 13:13).

Augustine concluded his treatise on faith, hope, and love with these words:

> But now there must be an end at last to this volume. And it is for yourself to judge whether you should call it a hand-book, or should use it as such. I, however, thinking that your zeal in Christ ought not to be despised, and believing and hoping all good of you in dependence on our Redeemer's help, and loving you very much as one of the members of His body, have, to the best of my ability, written this book for you on Faith, Hope, and Love. May its value be equal to its length.[4]

Amen.

APPENDIX

Question 58

Did Jesus possess faith, hope, and love?

Yes, as a true man, he was filled with all spiritual
virtues and graces, including faith, hope, and love.

Peter Lombard asks in his *Sentences* whether Christ had faith and
hope as he had charity (love). He comes to the conclusion that
Christ did not possess faith and hope.[1] In light of how I have understood faith, hope, and love in this book—including the earlier chapter on imitating Christ, the man of faith (see chap. 11)—I think we
must say of Christ that he possessed these three theological virtues.

Being fully human, Christ had the ability to grow in his graces:
"And Jesus increased in wisdom and in stature and in favor with
God and man" (Luke 2:52). We receive various graces from Christ,
such as faith, hope, and love, because he possessed these graces
preeminently in himself.

Jesus is distinguished as the pioneer of our faith since he himself had unwavering faith during the course of his life on earth (Heb. 12:2). The book of Hebrews explicitly connects faith (trust) to Christ, attributing to him these words: "I will put my trust in him" (Heb. 2:13). No one believed God's promises and lived his or her life in light of those promises like Jesus did (Heb. 10:37–38). Though his family doubted him, his disciples abandoned him, his friend denied him, and his fellow Jews rejected him, Jesus had faith to trust his Father, who would one day (at his resurrection) vindicate him (Isa. 50:6–9). Christ no doubt loved the words of Psalm 16:1, "Preserve me, O God, for in you I take refuge."

As one who had faith, he also necessarily had hope. He lived constantly with the hope of better things to come. His life was a life of humiliation, but he hoped for his exaltation (John 17). Unchangeable promises were made to Christ. As the faithful last Adam, Christ not only believed that he would one day be glorified in the presence of his Father at his right hand but also necessarily hoped for that day to arrive. If he did not hope for the promises made to him, then he surely was not truly human.

Christ had a particular hope in his own resurrection (see Psalm 16). He knew he would die, but he also knew he would be raised (Mark 10:33–34). In the pain and agony of Golgotha, Christ never lost hope that he would be vindicated. He never lost hope that his temporal sufferings would pale in comparison to the glory that would be given to him (see Rom. 8:18).

The threefold cord of Christ's life was completed by love. God is love, but Christ is love covered in flesh. Everything about Christ's life falls under the category of love. He had love for his disciples: "Now before the Feast of the Passover, when Jesus knew that his hour had come to depart out of this world to the Father, having loved his own who were in the world, he loved them to the end" (John 13:1). He had love for his enemies: "And Jesus said, 'Father, forgive them, for they know not what they do'" (Luke 23:34).

He had love for the crowds of needy people (Mark 6:34–44). But he had a special love for his Father: "I do as the Father has commanded me, so that the world may know that I love the Father" (John 14:31). Indeed, he explicitly connects his love toward the Father with keeping his Father's commandments. Jesus could not have endured all that he endured, as the obedient Son, if he did not have love for his Father.

Christ had to have trust in his Father, hope in his Father's promises, and love for his Father in order to bestow on us those graces that are first in him. We can say with great praise that we are "so thankful for the faith, hope, and love of Christ; no hope without them."

Catechism

PART 1   FAITH

1 What is the worst sin?
The worst (and first) sin is unbelief.

2 What is saving faith?
Saving faith is the Spirit-enabled embrace of and resting on our faithful God in Christ for the redemption offered by him through the promise of the gospel.

3 Where does faith come from?
Faith, while a human act, comes from God as a supernatural and empowered gift.

4 What does it mean that faith is supernatural?
That faith is supernatural means that it cannot be experienced according to the natural order of things, specifically the natural ability of man.

5 Are we justified by believing in the doctrine of justification by faith alone?
No, while faith requires an object, namely, Christ, we are justified through faith in him, not in all the details of this doctrine.

6 What does our faith lay hold of?
Our faith lays hold of Christ along with all the saving benefits that are graciously offered through union with him.

7 **Can we lose our justification?**
No, we cannot lose our justification, because it comes by faith alone and because Christ protects it by his intercession for us.

8 **Is faith our righteousness?**
No, faith is the sole instrument whereby God graciously imputes to us the righteousness of Christ.

9 **What is the principal exercise of faith?**
The contemplation of the glory of Christ is the principal exercise of faith.

10 **What is the principle of our obedience?**
Faith, by which we are sanctified, is the principle of our obedience.

11 **In addition to being the object of our faith, is Jesus also the pattern of our faith?**
This we happily affirm, for Jesus is the greatest example of believing ever.

12 **Can faith be increased and strengthened?**
Yes, faith may be increased and strengthened by the Spirit through the Word, sacraments, and prayer.

13 **Should those with saving faith fear God and tremble at his threats?**
Yes, those with saving faith should possess a filial fear and trembling that reveres God as Father and keeps them from a servile terror of him as Judge.

14 **Is there such a thing as false faith?**
Yes, many possess false faith, faith that may appear real but is not supernatural.

15 **What is Satan's goal in his assaults on God's children?**
Satan assaults God's children with the goal of getting them to forsake God and faith in him, especially through the neglect of the Word and prayer.

16 **How should we respond in the trials God sends us?**
We should respond by faith in trials, which come as gifts from a good, wise, and powerful God, as he refines and perfects our faith.

17 **Does true faith always persevere and end in victory?**
Yes, faith, as a supernatural gift of God, perseveres to the end in victory, only because of Jesus Christ, who can never fail.

PART 2   HOPE

18 **How is hope commonly understood?**
Hope is typically seen as the optimistic expectation that something will happen in this life or the one to come, but this must be distinguished from Christian hope.

19 **What is Christian hope?**
Christian hope is a Spirit-given virtue enabling us to joyfully expect things promised by God through Jesus Christ.

20 **What gives rise to Christian hope?**
Faith in God through Christ by the Spirit gives rise to Christian hope.

21 **Is hope necessary for the Christian?**
Yes, because we are born into a living hope through regeneration, this grace necessarily manifests itself in this life in expectation of good things from God.

22 **To whom is Christian hope given?**
God gives this grace of hope both individually to the Christian and corporately in the life of the church.

23 **How does hope relate to death?**
Hope prompts us to cling to the promise that when we die, we will be with Christ in paradise.

24 **What is the supreme object of Christian hope?**
The supreme object of Christian hope is Christ as seen face-to-face in his glory.

25 How does Christian hope relate to our future vision of Christ?
Our future vision of Christ necessitates the expectation for a resurrected body like his.

26 In what destination do we long to live forever?
We long to live forever in the new heavens and new earth, communing with the Father, Son, and Holy Spirit and with each other through the Spirit.

27 Of what use is hope in times of suffering?
In suffering, hope comforts our souls and allows us to live patiently while the church waits for her entrance into glory.

28 What hope do we have regarding the salvation of our children?
We have great hope regarding the salvation of our children, because a promise is made to them, and they belong to the Lord.

29 May we have hope regarding the death of infants?
A Christian parent may have a confident hope that his or her child dies in the Lord.

30 What duty flows out of Christian hope?
Those who hope in God purify themselves.

PART 3   LOVE

31 What is the foundation of the Christian religion?
The foundation of the Christian religion is the love of God toward his people through Christ and the love of his people for him.

32 What is love?
Love is a virtue that seeks union, satisfaction, and goodwill.

33 What is the guide to loving God and our neighbor?
The Ten Commandments are the guide to loving God and our neighbor.

34 How do we fail to show love for God?
We fail to show love for God by breaking his commandments.

35 **How do we show our love for God?**
As Christ did before us, we show our love for God by keeping his commandments.

36 **What makes our obedience acceptable to God?**
Obedience becomes acceptable to God when it is worked by the Spirit and motivated by love.

37 **How does faith work through love?**
Faith works through love by keeping the commandments of God.

38 **What is the context for our love?**
We love in the context of the church both those in the church and those outside the church.

39 **What is the chief end of our love to others?**
The chief end of our love to others is to glorify God and Christ by loving them first and foremost.

40 **How can we keep ourselves from idolatry, which manifests hatred toward God?**
We keep ourselves from idolatry by worshiping the triune God, which manifests our love toward him.

41 **What guards the church from false worship?**
The Bible alone as a sufficient rule for worshiping God guards us from that which is false.

42 **How should God's people regard themselves in the Christian life?**
God's people should regard themselves as his image bearers in their conduct and speech, whereby they hallow his name.

43 **Does God offer us a particular day in which we may rest and stir up our love for him and others?**
Yes, God has given us the Lord's Day, when the church gathers to worship, as a unique day for resting and stirring up our love for him and others.

44 How do we love those who are in a higher or lower position than ourselves?

We love our neighbors who are in a high or low estate by affording to them either proper respect and honor or fatherly/motherly care.

45 What obedience should Christian parents expect from their children?

Children must offer loving obedience to their parents "in the Lord."

46 Why are we to have love and respect for human life?

Because humans are made in the image of God.

47 How are we to show our love and respect for human life?

We show our love and respect for human life by doing everything we can to preserve human life and by refraining from anything that could unlawfully harm it.

48 What are our sexual duties in this life, and how does the fulfillment of such manifest love?

These duties include maintaining pure thoughts and actions and sexually satisfying our spouse out of love that prefers the other.

49 What is the primary mark of a Christian marriage?

The primary mark of a Christian marriage is love that reflects the union of Christ and the church.

50 Why is adultery such a heinous sin?

Adultery is so heinous because it betrays the faithful love of the Lord Jesus Christ, violates the marriage covenant, destroys the lives of innocent people, and involves several other sins against God and man.

51 How does love manifest itself in regard to our worldly goods and name?

Love manifests itself in regard to our worldly goods and name when expressed in a spirit of trust toward God and generosity toward man.

52 **How is our generosity in love to be shown in the local church?**
Generosity is shown in the local church by giving ourselves first to kingdom work.

53 **Why is lying so serious?**
Lying is so serious because love rejoices with the truth, while lying shows hatred.

54 **How do we show love with regard to our speech?**
We show love with regard to our speech when we speak the truth seasonably and in love at all times.

55 **What keeps us from an inordinate desire for the things of the world?**
We avoid an inordinate desire for the things of the world through our love for our heavenly Father and our knowledge that he knows what we need and gives good gifts to his children.

56 **Is love optional for Christians?**
No, love is not optional for Christians, for unless their love exceeds that of the scribes and Pharisees, they cannot enter the kingdom of heaven.

57 **Of faith, hope, and love, which is the greatest?**
Love is the greatest, because it alone will remain in eternity and because it makes us most like God.

APPENDIX

58 **Did Jesus possess faith, hope, and love?**
Yes, as a true man, he was filled with all spiritual virtues and graces, including faith, hope, and love.

Notes

PART 1   FAITH

Question 1

1. John Ball, *A Treatise of Faith* (London: for Edward Brewster, 1657), 202.
2. C. H. Spurgeon, "The Sin of Unbelief: A Sermon Delivered on Sunday Morning, January 14, 1855" (Pasadena, TX: Pilgrim, 1970), 12.

Question 2

1. Thomas Watson, *Body of Divinity* (Edinburgh: Banner of Truth, 1970), 216.

Question 3

1. Parts of this chapter are adapted from Mark Jones, "The Act and Habit of Faith in Relation to Union with Christ," in cooperation with and first published by the Alliance of Confessing Evangelicals at *reformation21* (blog), April 30, 2015, http://www.reformation21.org/blog/2015/04/the-act-habit-of-faith-union-w.php.
2. John Flavel, *The Works of John Flavel* (1820; repr., Edinburgh: Banner of Truth, 1968), 4:352–53.
3. Peter Bulkeley, *The Gospel-Covenant; or, the Covenant of Grace Opened* (London, 1646), 298.
4. Thomas Goodwin, *The Object and Acts of Justifying Faith*, in *The Works of Thomas Goodwin* (1864; repr., Grand Rapids, MI: Reformation Heritage Books, 2006), 8:273.
5. Goodwin, *Object and Acts of Justifying Faith*, in *Works*, 8:463.
6. Thomas Goodwin, "Exposition of Various Portions of the Epistle to the Ephesians," in *Works*, 2:404.
7. Herman Witsius, *Conciliatory or Irenical Animadversions on the Controversies Agitated in Britain, under the Unhappy Names of Antinomians and Neonomians*, trans. Thomas Bell (Glasgow: W. Lang, 1807), 68.

8. Martin Luther, quoted in Richard B. Gaffin Jr., *By Faith, Not By Sight: Paul and the Order of Salvation*, 2nd ed. (Phillipsburg, NJ: P&R, 2013), 119.
9. Goodwin, "Exposition of Various Portions of Ephesians," in *Works*, 2:404.
10. Goodwin, "Exposition of Various Portions of Ephesians," in *Works*, 2:412.

Question 4

1. John Calvin, *Institutes of the Christian Religion*, ed. John T. McNeill, trans. Ford Lewis Battles, Library of Christian Classics (Philadelphia: Westminster, 1960), 3.2.6.
2. Francis Turretin, *Institutes of Elenctic Theology*, ed. James T. Dennison Jr., trans. George Musgrave Giger (Phillipsburg, NJ: P&R, 1992), 1:62.
3. J. I. Packer, *A Quest for Godliness: The Puritan Vision of the Christian Life* (Wheaton, IL: Crossway, 1990), 82–83.
4. John Owen, *The Reason of Faith*, in *The Works of John Owen*, ed. William H. Goold (repr., Edinburgh: Banner of Truth, 1965–1968), 4:8.
5. Owen, *Reason of Faith*, in *Works*, 4:9.
6. Owen, *Reason of Faith*, in *Works*, 4:49.
7. Thomas Goodwin, *Of the Creatures, and the Condition of Their State by Creation*, in *The Works of Thomas Goodwin* (1863; repr., Grand Rapids, MI: Reformation Heritage Books, 2006), 7:63.
8. Calvin, *Institutes*, 3.2.6.
9. Tertullian, *De carne Christi liber. Treatise on the Incarnation*, ed. Ernest Evans (London: SPCK, 1956), 5.4.

Question 5

1. This chapter is adapted from Mark Jones, "Justification by Precision Alone?," in cooperation with and first published by the Alliance of Confessing Evangelicals at *reformation21* (blog), October 13, 2014, http://www.reformation21.org/blog/2014/10/justification-by-precision -alo.php.
2. John Owen, *The Doctrine of Justification by Faith*, in *The Works of John Owen*, ed. William H. Goold (repr., Edinburgh: Banner of Truth, 1965–1968), 5:163–64.
3. Owen, *Doctrine of Justification by Faith*, in *Works*, 5:63.
4. Owen, *Doctrine of Justification by Faith*, in *Works*, 5:164.
5. Owen, *Doctrine of Justification by Faith*, in *Works*, 5:164.

Question 6

1. This chapter is adapted from Mark Jones, "An Apologie," in cooperation with and first published by the Alliance of Confessing Evangelicals

at *reformation21* (blog), June 2, 2014, http://www.reformation21.org /blog/2014/06/an-apologie.php.

2. Francis Turretin, *Institutes of Elenctic Theology*, ed. James T. Dennison Jr., trans. George Musgrave Giger (Phillipsburg, NJ: P&R, 1992), 17.3.12.

3. Herman Witsius, *Conciliatory or Irenical Animadversions on the Controversies Agitated in Britain, under the Unhappy Names of Antinomians and Neonomians*, trans. Thomas Bell (Glasgow: W. Lang, 1807), 162.

4. George Downame, *A Treatise of Justification* (London: Felix Kyngston for Nicolas Bourne, 1633), 470.

5. Thomas Goodwin, *An Exposition of the Second Chapter of the Epistle to the Ephesians, Verses 1–11*, in *The Works of Thomas Goodwin* (1861; repr., Grand Rapids, MI: Reformation Heritage Books, 2006), 2:336.

6. Goodwin, *Exposition of the Second Chapter of Ephesians*, in *Works*, 2:336.

Question 7

1. This chapter is adapted from Mark Jones, "Can Justification Be Lost?," in cooperation with and first published by the Alliance of Confessing Evangelicals at *reformation21* (blog), October 20, 2015, http://www .reformation21.org/blog/2015/10/can-justification-be-lost.php.

2. I am still looking for a primary source that proves that Luther is the originator of the phrase, but the saying may still have come from him. For example, as early as 1654, William Eyre labels justification "*articulus stantis aut cadentis Ecclesiae*, as Luther calls it." Likewise, John Owen uses the "stands or falls" phrase when referring to justification as "*Articulus stantis aut cadentis Ecclesiae*," "the article by which the church stands or falls." Thus, Richard John Neuhaus wrongly argues that the "stands or falls" phrase did not originate until the eighteenth century. William Eyre, *Vindiciae justificationis gratuitae* (London, 1654), 17; John Owen, *The Doctrine of Justification by Faith through the Imputation of the Righteousness of Christ* (London, 1677), 83, 87; Richard John Neuhaus, "The Catholic Difference," in *Evangelicals and Catholics Together: Toward a Common Mission*, ed. Charles Colson and Richard John Neuhaus (Dallas: Word, 1995), 199. Owen goes on to say, "In my judgment, Luther spake the truth when he said; *amisso Articulo Justificationis, simul amissa est tota Doctrina Christiana*. The loss of the article of Justification, involves the loss of the whole Christian doctrine." Owen does not give a citation of Luther, notes Carl R. Trueman in "John Owen on Justification," in *Justified in Christ: God's*

Plan for Us in Justification, ed. K. Scott Oliphint (Fearn, Scotland: Mentor, 2007), 81.

3. John Owen, *The Doctrine of Justification by Faith*, in *The Works of John Owen*, ed. William H. Goold (repr., Edinburgh: Banner of Truth, 1965–1968), 5:290–91.

4. Owen, *Doctrine of Justification by Faith*, in *Works*, 5:292.

5. Owen, *Doctrine of Justification by Faith*, in *Works*, 5:237.

6. Owen, *Doctrine of Justification by Faith*, in *Works*, 5:293.

7. Owen, *Doctrine of Justification by Faith*, in *Works*, 5:294.

8. Owen, *Doctrine of Justification by Faith*, in *Works*, 5:311.

9. Owen, *Doctrine of Justification by Faith*, in *Works*, 5:292–93.

10. Owen, *Doctrine of Justification by Faith*, in *Works*, 5:145.

11. Thomas Goodwin, *Christ Set Forth*, in *The Works of Thomas Goodwin* (1862; repr., Grand Rapids, MI: Reformation Heritage Books, 2006), 4:63.

12. Goodwin, *Christ Set Forth*, in *Works*, 4:64.

Question 8

1. B. B. Warfield, *The Works of Benjamin B. Warfield* (Grand Rapids, MI: Baker, 1978), 2:505.

2. This chapter is adapted from Mark Jones, "Arminian vs. Reformed on Justification," in cooperation with and first published by the Alliance of Confessing Evangelicals at *reformation21* (blog), May 26, 2015, http://www.reformation21.org/blog/2015/05/arminian-versus-reformed-views.php.

3. Michael Horton, *The Christian Faith: A Systematic Theology for Pilgrims on the Way* (Grand Rapids, MI: Zondervan, 2011), 627.

4. G. P. van Itterzon, *Franciscus Gomarus* (1930; repr., Groningen: Bouma's Boekhuis, 1979), 375.

5. Herman Witsius, *The Economy of the Covenants between God and Man: Comprehending a Complete Body of Divinity* (repr., Grand Rapids, MI: Reformation Heritage Books, 2010), 3.8.51.

6. Arminius clearly struggled in coming to a settled view. As Aza Goudriaan says in his excellent essay on this topic, "While it is difficult to pin Arminius down on one particular view, it is obvious that he suggested in certain texts a justification because of the act of faith." "Justification by Faith and the Early Arminian Controversy," in *Scholasticism Reformed: Essays in Honour of Willem J. van Asselt*, ed. Maarten Wisse, Marcel Sarot, and Willemien Otten, Studies in Religion 14 (Leiden: Brill, 2010), 163; cf. Keith D. Stanglin and Thomas H. McCall, *Jacob Arminius: Theologian of Grace* (New York: Oxford University Press, 2013), 167–68. On the later Arminian rejection of the Reformed doc-

trine of the imputation of Christ's righteousness, see Adam Clarke, *Christian Theology* (London: Thomas and Son, 1835), 156, 158; John Fletcher, *Checks to Antinomianism*, 3rd American ed. (New York: J. Soule and T. Mason, 1820); Richard Watson, *Theological Institutes; or, A View of the Evidences, Doctrines, Morals, and Institutions of Christianity* (New York: Emory and Waugh, 1831), 300. Mildred Wynkoop also notes, "The idea of a transfer of righteousness from Christ to man (or imputed righteousness) is the exact antithesis of the biblical concept of holiness. It relieves man of the necessity of any real heart change." *Foundations of Wesleyan-Arminian Theology* (Kansas City, MO: Beacon Hill, 1967), 116.

7. Herman Bavinck, *Reformed Dogmatics*, vol. 4, *Holy Spirit, Church, and New Creation*, ed. John Bolt, trans. John Vriend (Grand Rapids, MI: Baker Academic, 2008), 211.

8. As quoted in Goudriaan, "Justification by Faith and the Early Arminian Controversy," 172.

9. William Perkins, *A Golden Chaine* (Cambridge: John Legat, 1600), 941.

Question 9

1. John Owen, *Meditations and Discourses on the Glory of Christ*, in *The Works of John Owen*, ed. William H. Goold (repr., Edinburgh: Banner of Truth, 1965–1968), 1:303.

2. Owen, *Meditations and Discourses*, in *Works*, 1:303.

3. Owen, *Meditations and Discourses*, in *Works*, 1:304.

4. Thomas Watson, *Body of Divinity* (Edinburgh: Banner of Truth, 1970), 219.

Question 10

1. Thomas Watson, *Body of Divinity* (Edinburgh: Banner of Truth, 1970), 219.

2. John Ball, *A Treatise of Faith* (London: for Edward Brewster, 1657), 198.

3. B. B. Warfield, *The Works of Benjamin B. Warfield* (Grand Rapids, MI: Baker, 1978), 2:486.

Question 11

1. This chapter is adapted from Mark Jones, "Is Jesus the Pattern for Our Faith?," in cooperation with and first published by the Alliance of Confessing Evangelicals at *reformation21* (blog), October 29, 2014, http://www.reformation21.org/blog/2014/10/did-jesus-live-by-faith.php.

2. Thomas Goodwin, *The Heart of Christ in Heaven towards Sinners on Earth*, in *The Works of Thomas Goodwin* (1862; repr., Grand Rapids, MI: Reformation Heritage Books, 2006), 4:9.

3. Herman Bavinck, *Reformed Dogmatics*, vol. 4, *Holy Spirit, Church, and New Creation*, ed. John Bolt, trans. John Vriend (Grand Rapids, MI: Baker Academic, 2008), 101.

4. As exemplified in the classic fictional expression of theological liberalism, Charles M. Sheldon, *In His Steps* (Chicago: Advance, 1896).

5. Thomas Goodwin, *Christ Set Forth*, in *Works*, 4:9.

6. Goodwin, *Christ Set Forth*, in *Works*, 4:9.

7. John Owen, *An Exposition of the Epistle to the Hebrews*, ed. William H. Goold (repr., Edinburgh: Banner of Truth, 1991), 3:430.

8. John Calvin, *Commentary on the Epistle of Paul the Apostle to the Hebrews*, trans. John Owen, in vol. 22 of *Calvin's Commentaries* (repr., Grand Rapids, MI: Baker, 1999), 68.

9. Richard Sibbes, *A Description of Christ*, in *The Complete Works of Richard Sibbes* (1862; repr., Edinburgh: Banner of Truth, 2004), 1:18.

10. Bavinck, *Reformed Dogmatics*, vol. 3, *Sin and Salvation in Christ*, 312.

11. John Owen, *A Declaration of the Glorious Mystery of the Person of Christ*, in *The Works of John Owen*, ed. William H. Goold (repr., Edinburgh: Banner of Truth, 1965–1968), 1:170.

12. Geerhardus Vos, *Grace and Glory: Sermons Preached in the Chapel of Princeton Theological Seminary* (Grand Rapids, MI: Reformed, 1922), 104.

Question 12

1. Parts of this chapter are adapted from Mark Jones, "The Difficulty of Prayer (and a Solution)," in cooperation with and first published by the Alliance of Confessing Evangelicals at *reformation21* (blog), September 29, 2015, http://www.reformation21.org/blog/2015/09/the-difficulty-of-prayer-and-a.php.

2. John Calvin, *Institutes of the Christian Religion*, ed. John T. McNeill, trans. Ford Lewis Battles, Library of Christian Classics (Philadelphia: Westminster, 1960), 3.2.31.

3. Thomas Goodwin, *The Heart of Christ in Heaven towards Sinners on Earth*, in *The Works of Thomas Goodwin* (1862; repr., Grand Rapids, MI: Reformation Heritage Books, 2006), 4:93–150.

4. John Ball, *A Treatise of Faith* (London: for Edward Brewster, 1657), 402.

Question 13

1. Parts of this chapter are adapted from Mark Jones, "Does the Gospel Threaten?," in cooperation with and first published by the Alliance of Confessing Evangelicals at *reformation21* (blog), March 23, 2015, http://www.reformation21.org/blog/2015/03/does-the-gospel-threaten.php.

2. William Ames, *The Marrow of Theology*, trans. and ed. John D. Eusden (1968; repr., Grand Rapids, MI: Baker, 1997), 242.

3. *Actes du Synode National Tenu à Dordrecht*, trans. Richard Jean de Nerée (Leiden: Elsevir, 1624), 1:507. My translation.

4. Dolfe te Velde, ed., *Synopsis Purioris Theologiae, Synopsis of a Purer Theology: Latin Text and English Translation*, vol. 1, *Disputations 1–23*, trans. Riemer A. Faber, Latin text ed. Rein Ferwerda (Leiden: Brill, 2015), 567.

5. John Owen, *An Exposition of the Epistle to the Hebrews*, ed. William H. Goold (repr., Edinburgh: Banner of Truth, 1991), 3:285.

6. Owen, *An Exposition of the Epistle to the Hebrews*, 3:286.

7. John Murray, *Principles of Conduct: Aspects of Biblical Conduct* (Grand Rapids, MI: Eerdmans, 1971), 236–37.

Question 14

1. John Calvin, *Commentaries on the Epistle of Paul the Apostle to the Hebrews*, trans. and ed. John Owen (Edinburgh, 1853), 138 (on Heb. 6:4).

2. Robert Rollock, *Select Works of Robert Rollock*, ed. William M. Gunn (Edinburgh: The Wodrow Society, 1841), 1:207.

3. R. Fowler White, "Covenant and Apostasy," in *The Auburn Avenue Theology, Pros and Cons: Debating the Federal Vision*, ed. E. Calvin Beisner (Fort Lauderdale, FL: Knox Theological Seminary, 2003), 214.

Question 16

1. Thomas Watson, *A Divine Cordial: An Exposition of Romans 8:28* (1663; repr., Counted Faithful, 2014), Kindle edition, chap. 2.

2. Watson, *Divine Cordial*, chap. 2.

3. Joseph Caryl, *An Exposition with Practical Applications upon . . . Job* (1644–1646; repr., Grand Rapids, MI: Reformation Heritage Books, 2001), 1:190.

PART 2   HOPE

Question 18

1. John Angell James, *The Christian Graces: Faith, Hope, and Love* (London: Hamilton Adams, 1860), 288.

Question 19

1. Thomas Aquinas, *Summa Theologiae* (Lander, WY: Aquinas Institute for the Study of Sacred Doctrine, 2012), 2.17.2.

2. William Ames, *The Marrow of Theology*, trans. and ed. John D. Eusden (1968; repr., Grand Rapids, MI: Baker, 1997), 246–47.

Question 20

1. Herman Ridderbos, *Paul: An Outline of His Theology* (Grand Rapids, MI: Eerdmans, 1975), 248.

2. J. Gresham Machen, *What Is Faith?* (1925; repr., Edinburgh: Banner of Truth, 1996), 231.

Question 21

1. Geerhardus Vos, "A Sermon on 1 Peter 1:3–5" (unpublished sermon, preached at Princeton Theological Seminary, November 13, 1904), *Kerux: The Journal of Northwest Theological Seminary* 1, no. 2 (1986): 4–17, accessed November 19, 2016, http://www.kerux.com /doc/0102A1.asp. The words here are transcribed from Vos's personal sermon notebook deposited in Heritage Hall of Calvin Theological Seminary in Grand Rapids, Michigan.

Question 22

1. See the appendix on the question of Christ's faith, hope, and love.
2. Peter Lombard, *The Sentences*, Book 3, *On the Incarnation of the Word*, trans. Giulio Silano, Mediaeval Sources in Translation 45 (Toronto: Pontifical Institute of Mediaeval Studies, 2010), 111.

Question 23

1. Thomas Adams, *The Works of Thomas Adams* (1862; repr., Eureka, CA: Tanski, 1998), 2:277.
2. John Angell James, *The Christian Graces: Faith, Hope, and Love* (London: Hamilton Adams, 1860), 306–7.
3. John Owen, *Meditations and Discourses on the Glory of Christ*, in *The Works of John Owen*, ed. William H. Goold (repr., Edinburgh: Banner of Truth, 1965–1968), 1:273.

Question 25

1. Parts of this chapter are adapted from Mark Jones, "Christ's Body and Affections in Heaven," in cooperation with and first published by the Alliance of Confessing Evangelicals at *reformation21* (blog), November 19, 2015, http://www.reformation21.org/blog/2015/11/christs -body-and-affections-in.php.
2. Thomas Goodwin, *The Heart of Christ in Heaven towards Sinners on Earth*, in *The Works of Thomas Goodwin* (1862; repr., Grand Rapids, MI: Reformation Heritage Books, 2006), 4:144.
3. Goodwin, *Heart of Christ*, in *Works*, 4:145.
4. Goodwin, *Heart of Christ*, in *Works*, 4:146.

Question 27

1. John Owen, *On the Dominion of Sin and Grace*, in *The Works of John Owen*, ed. William H. Goold (repr., Edinburgh: Banner of Truth, 1965–1968), 7:322.

2. Thomas Adams, *The Works of Thomas Adams* (1862; repr., Eureka, CA: Tanski, 1998), 2:277.

Question 29

1. This chapter is adapted from Mark Jones, "The Loss of Infants: What Is Their Destiny?," in cooperation with and first published by the Alliance of Confessing Evangelicals at *reformation21* (blog), July 28, 2015, http://www.reformation21.org/blog/2015/07/infants-dying-in -infancy-what.php.
2. Charles H. Spurgeon, "Infant Salvation: A Sermon," in *The New Park Street and Metropolitan Tabernacle Pulpit* (London: Passmore and Alabaster, 1862), 7:506.
3. Joyce G. Baldwin, *1 and 2 Samuel: An Introduction and Commentary*, Tyndale Old Testament Commentaries 8 (Downers Grove, IL: Inter-Varsity Press, 1988), 257.

Question 30

1. Jonathan Edwards, "Concerning Efficacious Grace," in *The Works of Jonathan Edwards*, ed. Edward Hickman (1834; repr., Edinburgh: Banner of Truth, 1974), vol. 2, chap. 4, §64.
2. Herman Bavinck, *Reformed Dogmatics*, vol. 3, *Sin and Salvation in Christ*, ed. John Bolt, trans. John Vriend (Grand Rapids, MI: Baker Academic, 2006), 3:243.
3. Bavinck, *Reformed Dogmatics*, 3:252.
4. Bavinck, *Reformed Dogmatics*, 3:252.
5. Bavinck, *Reformed Dogmatics*, 3:253.
6. Thomas Manton, *The Complete Works of Thomas Manton* (Worthington, PA: Maranatha, 1970), 3:159.

PART 3   LOVE

Question 31

1. Geerhardus Vos, *Redemptive History and Biblical Interpretation: The Shorter Writings of Geerhardus Vos*, ed. Richard B. Gaffin (Phillipsburg, NJ: P&R, 2001), 298.
2. Charles H. Spurgeon, "Love: A Sermon," in *The New Park Street Pulpit* (London: Passmore and Alabaster, 1894), 5:35.
3. Martin Luther, *Martin Luther's Basic Theological Writings*, ed. Timothy F. Lull (Minneapolis: Fortress, 1989), 32.
4. Luther, *Martin Luther's Basic Theological Writings*, 48.

5. Augustine, "Homilies on the First Epistle of John," in *Nicene and Post-Nicene Fathers*, ed. Philip Schaff (Grand Rapids, MI: Eerdmans, 1956), 7:503.

6. Anselm, *Proslogion*, in *Eerdmans' Book of Christian Classics: A Treasury of Christian Writings through the Centuries* (Grand Rapids, MI: Eerdmans, 1985), 27.

Question 32

1. Peter Lombard, *The Sentences*, Book 3, *On the Incarnation of the Word*, trans. Giulio Silano, Mediaeval Sources in Translation 45 (Toronto: Pontifical Institute of Mediaeval Studies, 2010), 113.

2. William Ames, *The Marrow of Theology*, trans. and ed. John D. Eusden (1968; repr., Grand Rapids, MI: Baker, 1997), 250.

3. Ames, *The Marrow of Theology*, 250.

4. These points summarize the discussion in Ames, *The Marrow of Theology*, 250–51.

5. Ames, *The Marrow of Theology*, 252.

6. Jonathan Edwards, *Charity and Its Fruits*, ed. Tryon Edwards (Philadelphia: Presbyterian Board of Publication, 1874), 4.

Question 33

1. Augustine, "Homilies on the First Epistle of John," in *Nicene and Post-Nicene Fathers*, ed. Philip Schaff (Grand Rapids, MI: Eerdmans, 1956), 7:506.

2. Here I am indebted to the argument made by Richard B. Gaffin Jr. See "Pentecost: Before and After," in *Kerux: The Journal of Northwest Theological Seminary* 10, no. 2 (1995): 3–24.

3. Here I make use of Sinclair Ferguson, *Devoted to God: Blueprints for Sanctification* (Edinburgh: Banner of Truth, 2016), 176–77.

Question 34

1. William Ames, *The Marrow of Theology*, trans. and ed. John D. Eusden (1968; repr., Grand Rapids, MI: Baker, 1997), 253.

Question 35

1. This chapter is adapted from Mark Jones, "Christ Kept the 10 Commandments," in cooperation with and first published by the Alliance of Confessing Evangelicals at *reformation21* (blog), April 6, 2015, http://www.reformation21.org/blog/2015/04/christ-kept-the-10 -commandment-1.php.

2. William Ames, *The Marrow of Theology*, trans. and ed. John D. Eusden (1968; repr., Grand Rapids, MI: Baker, 1997), 252.

Question 36

1. Augustine, "Homilies on the First Epistle of John," in *Nicene and Post-Nicene Fathers*, ed. Philip Schaff (Grand Rapids, MI: Eerdmans, 1956), 7:503.
2. Augustine, "Homilies on the First Epistle of John," in *Nicene and Post-Nicene Fathers*, 7:505.

Question 37

1. William Ames, *The Marrow of Theology*, trans. and ed. John D. Eusden (1968; repr., Grand Rapids, MI: Baker, 1997), 253.
2. Richard B. Gaffin Jr., *By Faith, Not By Sight: Paul and the Order of Salvation*, 2nd ed. (Phillipsburg, NJ: P&R, 2013), 119.
3. John Calvin, *Institutes of the Christian Religion*, ed. John T. McNeill, trans. Ford Lewis Battles, Library of Christian Classics (Philadelphia: Westminster, 1960), 3.11.20.
4. Anthony Burgess, *Vindiciae legis: or, A vindication of the morall law and the covenants, from the Errours of Papists, Arminians, Socinians, and more especially, Antinomians* (London: T. Underhill, 1646), 188.

Question 38

1. Cyprian of Carthage, *The Unity of the Catholic Church* (New York: Newman, 1956), 48 (§6).
2. John Calvin, *Institutes of the Christian Religion*, ed. John T. McNeill, trans. Ford Lewis Battles, Library of Christian Classics (Philadelphia: Westminster, 1960), 4.1.1.
3. C. S. Lewis, *The Four Loves* (New York: Harcourt, Brace, Jovanovich, 1960), 169.
4. Jonathan Edwards, *Charity and Its Fruits*, in *The Works of Jonathan Edwards*, ed. Edward Hickman (1834; repr., London: Banner of Truth, 1969), 24.

Question 39

1. David K. Naugle, *Reordered Love, Reordered Lives: Learning the Deep Meaning of Happiness* (Grand Rapids, MI: Eerdmans, 2008), 133.
2. William Ames, *The Marrow of Theology*, trans. and ed. John D. Eusden (1968; repr., Grand Rapids, MI: Baker, 1997), 77.
3. Jonathan Edwards, *Charity and Its Fruits*, in *The Works of Jonathan Edwards*, ed. Edward Hickman (1834; repr., London: Banner of Truth, 1969), 6.

Question 40
 1. This chapter is adapted from Mark Jones, "Worship," with permission of and first published by Ligonier Ministries, *Tabletalk Magazine*, November 1, 2011, http://www.ligonier.org/learn/articles/worship/.
 2. John Piper, *Let the Nations Be Glad! The Supremacy of God in Missions* (Grand Rapids, MI: Baker, 1993), 11.

Question 41
 1. Godefridus Udemans, *The Practice of Faith, Hope, and Love*, trans. Annemie Godbehere (Grand Rapids, MI: Reformation Heritage Books, 2012), 243.

Question 43
 1. Thomas Watson, *The Ten Commandments* (Edinburgh: Banner of Truth, 1965), 105.

Question 47
 1. Godefridus Udemans, *The Practice of Faith, Hope, and Love*, trans. Annemie Godbehere (Grand Rapids, MI: Reformation Heritage Books, 2012), 333.

Question 48
 1. This chapter is adapted from Mark Jones, "Masturbation: The Unforgivable Sin?," in cooperation with and first published by the Alliance of Confessing Evangelicals at *reformation21* (blog), August 19, 2014, http://www.reformation21.org/blog/2014/08/masturbation-the-unforgivable.php.
 2. Jochem Douma, *The Ten Commandments: Manual for the Christian Life* (Phillipsburg, NJ: P&R, 1996), 263.

Question 49
 1. *Catechism of the Catholic Church* (New York: Doubleday, 1994), 628, par. 2365, quoted in Mark A. Noll and Carolyn Nystrom, *Is the Reformation Over? An Evangelical Assessment of Contemporary Roman Catholicism* (Grand Rapids, MI: Baker Academic, 2005), 128.

Question 50
 1. Thomas Watson, *The Ten Commandments* (Edinburgh: Banner of Truth, 1965), 155.
 2. Watson, *The Ten Commandments*, 156.

Question 51
 1. William Shakespeare, *Othello* (Logan, IA: Perfection Learning Corporation, 2004), 169 (3.3).

Question 52

1. *The Book of Church Order of the Presbyterian Church in America*, 6th ed. (Lawrenceville, GA: Office of the Stated Clerk of the General Assembly of the Presbyterian Church in America, 2016), 57.5, http://www.pcaac.org/resources/bco/.

Question 53

1. Thomas Watson, *The Ten Commandments* (Edinburgh: Banner of Truth, 1965), 169.

Question 54

1. Godefridus Udemans, *The Practice of Faith, Hope, and Love*, trans. Annemie Godbehere (Grand Rapids, MI: Reformation Heritage Books, 2012), 460.

2. Quoted in Udemans, *The Practice of Faith, Hope, and Love*, 460.

Question 55

1. In Joy Davidman, *Smoke on the Mountain*, repr. ed. (Louisville: Westminster John Knox, 2007), 120.

Question 57

1. Peter Lombard, *The Sentences*, Book 3, *On the Incarnation of the Word*, trans. Giulio Silano, Mediaeval Sources in Translation 45 (Toronto: Pontifical Institute of Mediaeval Studies, 2010), 110.

2. Thomas Adams, *The Works of Thomas Adams* (1862; repr., Eureka, CA: Tanski, 1998), 2:274.

3. Jonathan Edwards, "Heaven Is a World of Love," in *The Sermons of Jonathan Edwards: A Reader*, ed. Wilson H. Kimnach, Kenneth P. Minkema, and Douglas A. Sweeney (New Haven, CT: Yale University Press, 1999), 245.

4. Augustine, *Enchiridion: On Faith, Hope, and Love* (Londonderry, 1887), 192.

APPENDIX

1. Peter Lombard, *The Sentences*, Book 3, *On the Incarnation of the Word*, trans. Giulio Silano, Mediaeval Sources in Translation 45 (Toronto: Pontifical Institute of Mediaeval Studies, 2010), 97, 112.

General Index

Abel, 194
abortion, 139
abounding in hope, 103
Abraham
    faith of, 60–64, 90
    hope of, 105–6
acquisition of life, 44–45
act-habit distinction, 31–34
Adam
    broke all Ten Commandments,
        163–66, 167
    as prophet, priest, and king,
        129, 164
    unbelief of, 21, 75
Adams, Thomas, 113, 132,
    247–48
adoption, 43, 131, 143, 181–82
adultery, 216–17, 223–25
afflictions, 86
Ames, William, 73, 102, 155, 163,
    167, 175, 184
anger, 214–15
Anselm of Canterbury, 153
antinomianism, 34
anxiety, 69
apostasy, 80–81, 135
Apostles' Creed, 15
Arminianism, 51–52, 264n6(2)
Arminius, Jacob, 51–52, 264n6(2)
arrogance, 215
asceticism, 239

assent, 27
assurance, 26, 70
Athanasius, 234–35
Augustine, 13, 14, 118, 151, 158,
    172–73, 183, 250
authority and submission, 202–4

Baldwin, Joyce, 140
Ball, John, 23, 63, 70
baptism, 70, 98–99, 193, 223
Bavinck, Herman, 65, 68, 143–44
beatific vision, 46
Bertius, Petrus, 53–54
blessings in this life, 99
boasting, 215
Bulkeley, Peter, 32
Burgess, on the law, 177
"by faith alone," 176

Cain, 194, 233
Calvin, John, 36, 38, 67, 70,
    78–79, 176
Canons of Dort, 75, 138, 140
catechetical instruction, 15–16
ceremonial law, 159
character, produces hope, 111, 130
chief end of man, 183–84
children
    as heirs of covenant promises,
        133–35
    obedience to parents, 205–8

274

Scripture Index

Scripture Index

Also Available from Mark Jones

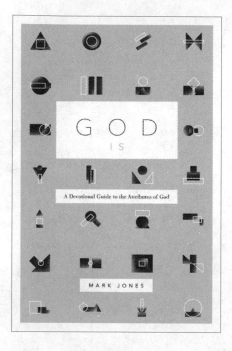

With brevity and clarity, Mark Jones makes the doctrine of God accessible through 26 devotional chapters on the attributes of God—with a specific focus on how each of the attributes is seen most fully in Christ and impacts the life of every Christian.

For more information, visit crossway.org.